Foreword

Kristin Fontana

Oh la luna, what would we ever do without the Moon? She is a guiding light in the best of times as well as in the most challenging of turns. She submerges us into those feeling pools in order to clear the unwanted, so our Soul can evolve into more productive seas.

The Moon is analogous to a river. When you surrender freely to the tides, your Soul will follow the path of least resistance as you find your way back home to the sea.

The Moon governs the emotional body, and it is within these watery worlds where the Soul experiences that visceral feeling of what it means to be human; emotions of joy, grief, love, loss, growth and pain. The emotions let us know intimately where we are at any point on the evolutionary journey and how we are directly and deeply navigating the tides we are traveling within. When we tap into our inherent emotional strength, it can propel us further on the Soul's intended path, and allow for a greater manifestation of our desires to occur.

On the flipside, the fear of the unknown can interrupt those natural tides, as no Soul enjoys feeling insecure, so the tendency to resist the water and repeat key lessons on the journey can also play out as a theme.

In Evolutionary Astrology, it is taught that the Soul can only evolve through the emotional door, that there is a limit to what the mind can access, and ultimately there is no avoiding these waters if you wish to experience forward momentum.

The Moon rules the sign of Cancer, the first of the water elements, i.e. Cancer, Scorpio Pisces. As an individual enters the emotional realm, it is there where the Soul can access the deep that leads to higher reaches of self actualization and greater degrees of purpose and connection.

The Moon and its Nodes in Evolutionary Astrology is incredibly unique in that Deva not only gives rise and depth to understanding the nature of the natal Moon in the birth chart through all the houses and astrological signs, she addresses the power of the lunar trinity to facilitate the Soul's evolution. This includes the natal placement of the Moon, as well as the nodes of the Moon. The natal position of the Moon symbolizes the emotional body that the individual chose in this life to promote Soul intended growth. The South Node of the Moon reflects the ego the Soul chose in the past to allow for evolution, and the North Node of the Moon points to the emotional energy that the individual needs in order to assist in the progression of the Soul.

As Souls we are all at different places on the wheel, so to speak, which means that these lunar placements will manifest differently depending on what stage of evolution an individual finds itself within. This is critical in chart interpretation to understand how the Moon and the Nodes are operating in any given life so the astrologer can validate to the client one's emotional process and point to steps that will allow the Soul to emerge more empowered and conscious of its footsteps.

Deva takes you on a journey with the Moon through the houses and signs, bringing light and understanding to the many levels of the emotional body and how the various archetypes are inwardly experienced and outwardly expressed. In addition, she shares examples of how that Moon is expressed in different stages of evolution, to allow for an awareness of what it looks and feels like for these lunar energies to evolve. This is the only book available to my knowledge that addresses the evolution of the Moon with this degree of meaningful significance..

The Moon

and its Nodes in Evolutionary Astrology

The Moon

and its Nodes in Evolutionary Astrology

Deva Green

THE WESSEX ASTROLOGER

Published in 2022 by
The Wessex Astrologer Ltd
PO Box 9307
Swanage
BH19 9BF

For a full list of our titles go to www.wessexastrologer.com

ISBN 9781910531792

Cover design by Fiona Bowring at Bowring Creative

With thanks to Astrolabe Inc (alabe.com) for the use of Solar Fire software
in the creation of horoscope charts

A catalogue record for this book is available at The British Library

Table of Contents

Lastly, this lunar guide offers in depth chart examples of well known people who are at different stages of evolution utilizing the Evolutionary Astrology Pluto paradigm. In addition to a thorough interpretation of the Moon and the nodal positions, Deva answers the bigger question, "Why". Why this Moon and why this journey? Thus, the reader can observe in living, breathing color how these lunar forces operate and are expressed.

When we are honoring what the Moon is trying to teach us, the Soul can more effortlessly evolve along the evolutionary continuum versus the tendency of being stuck in the same emotional nook time and time again. We are also learning more often than not, that "if it feels right, it is right", even when it hurts, for when we surrender to that watery current the river always flows true to course.

As Souls we are driven to express our truest selves out in the world, but we are also on an inner journey back home to our deepest selves, so that we may experience a greater feeling of wholeness, and thus holiness. If we can slip into those waters free of unwanted clothing, layers of holding that will create a drag on our energy and life force, we will discover that our greatest growth starts when have the courage to be vulnerable, the secret that will then lead to our ultimate strength.

The Moon and its Nodes in Evolutionary Astrology shows you the way.

Introduction

A main theme, or central principle, within evolutionary astrology is the transition from our past to our evolutionary future. All of us experience a natural tension and sense of insecurity when faced with change and the release of past emotional patterns that are preventing further growth and creating blocks with respect to our evolution. In this chapter we will discuss how this evolutionary shift from past to future is reflected by the natal Moon and the lunar nodes in the birth chart.

In the birth chart, the position of the natal Moon indicates how we will cope, on a day-to-day basis, with the stress caused by releasing these patterns and blocks, and how we will integrate the changes that signify the transition from the past to the future. In the course of these changes the Soul progressively shifts emotional security from external sources of all sorts to an internal state of security; a state of self-security. Our self-image naturally changes through this process. Ultimately, the gravitational pull away from past patterns is a reflection of the growing push towards recovering our original root or nature as we evolve, or return, back to the Source of All Things. In essence, we must all cultivate an inner space or state of emotional security instead of remaining stuck in outdated sources of external dependency. We must make this shift so that we can move with the natural flow of the evolutionary tides for the life as we reunite with God/dess and return to our origins.

In the natal chart, the South Node of the Moon corresponds to the past self-image of the Soul, the natal Moon corresponds to the current self-image of Soul, and the North Node corresponds to the forming, or developing, self-image of the Soul. The natural law of the trinity: past, present and future, is reflected in these symbols. This natural law is a core principle upon which evolutionary astrology is founded. In the context of the Moon and the lunar nodes, the South Node represents the past, the Moon represents the present, and the North Node represents the future. As mentioned previously, the natal Moon serves as a bridge between the evolutionary past and the future.

As JWG teaches, in every life the Soul creates an ego through which the current evolutionary intentions are integrated. The ego is structured in such a way as to support the ongoing evolution of the Soul, and thus serves as an integration function within consciousness. In other words, the Soul creates a distinct self-image, or personal lens, through which we then know and see ourselves. It is our "inner home," so to speak, how we live within ourselves on an emotional level. The analogy that is given to us in the Pluto material to illustrate this principle is that the ego is similar to a lens on a movie projector. Without the lens there would be diffused images of light. Without the ego we would not be able to speak our own names. The core point to remember within this is that we cannot get rid of our ego as so many spiritual teachings would suggest. From my view, the ultimate intention of spiritual life is to re-align the ego through merging with God/dess.

This archetype indicates the dynamics that the Soul will identify with for emotional and security purposes on a subjective level. It corresponds to the early childhood environment, and to the biological mother or the key parental figure(s) who provide the most emotional nurturing and security. A key aspect within this is that of self-nurturing. In my view, the capacity to self-nurture reflects the shift from external to internal security because we are learning to emotionally support ourselves and meet our own needs from within instead of deriving this from external sources.

Over a great period of evolutionary time the center of gravity within consciousness shifts from the ego to the Soul. The analogy that is used to illustrate this principle is the wave upon the sea. If the center of gravity of consciousness is centered in the individual wave, the ego, then I am identified as a separate entity: the individual wave. If the center of gravity within consciousness is centered within the sea, Soul, then the ego no longer identifies itself as being separate from its own Soul, or separate from its ultimate origins: the Source of All Things.

In essence, the self-image and emotional structure within the Soul undergoes a metamorphosis as we merge and re-unite with the God/dess. This process is reflected in the natural water trinity in the zodiac: Cancer, Scorpio and Pisces. The Cancer archetype symbolizes the ego, Scorpio symbolizes metamorphosis, and Pisces symbolizes union with the Source; **an important point here is that evolution occurs through the emotional body.**

The Moon and the lunar nodes reflect the specific areas where we will experience the emotional pull to the past, South Node, and the push towards the future, North Node, as it relates to the current moment in time, the Moon. The self-image naturally changes correspondingly.

In so doing, the Soul releases past patterns of external emotional security through its union with the Universal Source, and it is often through the progressive removal of all external dependencies that this core lesson is learned; that true security can only be found and cultivated from within ourselves via a connection to the Universal Source.

The anima/animus dynamic is reflected by the Moon as well. The Soul is intrinsically both male and female yet will preponderantly manifest in one gender versus the other. Over a great period of evolutionary time we must integrate both the inner male and inner female equally.

It is important to note the impact of gender assignment in the context of the Moon's correspondence to the self-image. To clarify this point, JWG often used the example of a woman with a Moon in Aries, and a man with a Moon in Pisces. Relative to prevailing cultural conditioning women are expected to play the traditional stay-at-home female role and men are expected to play the traditional macho male role in patriarchal societies. However, the woman with an Aries Moon will not see herself in this light. Similarly, the man with the Moon in Pisces will not see himself as a macho Man; it will take tremendous courage for a woman to walk as an equal in the world and to challenge a man in a similar field where men are deemed as being worth more, just as it will take great courage for a man to be emotionally sensitive and open in a world where boys are told not to cry. As mentioned before, one must become self-secure before integration of the anima/animus can take hold.

The South Node symbolizes the distinct prior life lens and resulting self-image that the Soul created in order to actualize the core desires of the evolutionary past symbolized by natal Pluto. It signifies how the Soul has necessarily oriented to reality in order to consciously emotionally integrate the core dynamics of the past (Pluto). The South Node symbolizes the specific dynamics that will represent emotional security on a subjective level, and the conscious emotional patterns that we must often return to habitually because of security derived from them.

The Moon corresponds to self-image, or personal lens, and resulting emotional structure of the Soul. The natal position of the Moon signifies the distinct personal lens the Soul will create to work through and cope with the natural tension felt in the push away from the past (South Node) and towards the future (North Node) in the present moment (Moon). In essence, it acts as a bridge between the emotional shift from our past and the future. It represents the areas in which the individual will feel the most drawn to self-nurture and emotionally support him- or herself through the stress of the transition away from past patterns of external emotional security towards self-security. In this light, the natal Moon corresponds to the specific dynamics through which the Soul will foster an internalized state of security, and work through the feelings of vulnerability and insecurity that such changes often create. This is the pathway, or gateway, through which we progressively shift emotional security from external sources to internal and embrace our natural roots.

The North Node reflects the evolving, or forming, self-lens and emotional structure of the Soul. Just as the Soul has created a prior life self-image to actualize the evolutionary intentions of the past (Pluto), so too will the Soul create a developing, or forming, self-image and distinct personal lens through which the current life's intentions will be actualized (Pluto's polarity point). In other words, the evolving emotional structure/ self-image of the Soul is put together in order to facilitate the ongoing growth needs of the Soul as it returns to Source. We progressively create an inner space of self security as we release past emotional patterns that are causing stagnation and non-growth, and nurture our connection to the Universal Source. Our personal lens, or how we see and know ourselves on an egocentric level, naturally shifts as a result of such evolution. The position of the North Node corresponds with the specific self-image the Soul will create in order to consciously manifest the current life intentions as indicated by Pluto's polarity point; it indicates the developing self-image that reflects the progressive merging and return to God/dess.

The way these core points work out in a life can be seen in the context of a client's case study in Chapter 3.

Chapter 1

The Natal Moon

In this chapter we will focus on the primary archetype of the natal Moon through the signs. The natal Moon corresponds to the specific self-image and emotional structure that the Soul has created in the current life. In other words, it symbolizes the specific personal lens through which we consciously see ourselves. It reflects our emotional nature, our "inner home," and where we inwardly dwell; where we will feel most drawn to nurture ourselves, to cultivate internal security, and where we are most vulnerable as we experience the insecurity of the change experienced by the pull away from the past emotional patterns that are inhibiting further growth.

As Jeffrey Wolf Green teaches, each Soul creates a distinct self-image (ego) that is structured to support the integration of the current life's evolutionary/karmic intentions. This is because our specific self-image serves as a means to emotionally facilitate the evolution back to origins, or root, as we begin to consciously merge with God/dess.

As previously discussed, the Moon acts as a bridge between the past (South Node) and the future (North Node). The natural tension between the past and the future is felt by the natal Moon; a key point within this is that we must embrace the insecurity that arises when we are in times of evolutionary transition, and must change patterns that are no longer supporting further evolution. In essence, it reflects how we will secure and support ourselves through these changes, and progressively shift emotional security from external to internal.

As we discuss the Moon in each sign please remember that these are general descriptions of the core evolutionary intentions and we must include the other mitigating factors to arrive at an accurate understanding of the Moon in any natal chart. These factors include: gender, economic class, cultural/religious conditioning and evolutionary condition.

Moon in Aries: The Moon in Aries reflects a self-image and inner emotional nature that is primarily rooted in the need for self-discovery and personal freedom. In essence, the need is to break free from the past so that a new evolutionary cycle can begin. As such, these individuals are typically highly independent, and will need the emotional freedom to initiate whatever experiences are deemed necessary to put this new cycle into motion. These Souls embody the spirit of the warrior.

The reason for this is that self-discovery occurs through the initiation of actions on an instinctual basis. In other words, experience is the vehicle through which self-discovery and development of the identity can occur. Individuals with this natal Moon need the freedom to feel any emotion without restriction; to feel without limits.

The sign of Aries signifies that a brand new cycle of evolutionary growth is underway. It is a cardinal archetype which reflects the need to initiate change. Cardinal archetypes manifest as "two steps forward, one step back." The Soul will take two steps towards change, then become insecure relative to the change and take one step back. With the Moon in Aries this can be expressed as jumping two steps ahead of oneself and then jumping back one step. Emotional integration occurs through the initiation of action, and the resulting feedback or response. This is reflected by the natural square between Capricorn and Aries.

The self-image and underlying emotional nature is founded on the need to maintain an essential freedom and independence. A sense of special destiny is felt with what is to come, a new evolutionary cycle, and the resulting emotional need is for the freedom to act upon whatever experiences are deemed necessary to discover what the new cycle is about.

In a natural expression, there is an inherent courage to pioneer in new and unexplored fields, to move things forward from the past in an almost emotionally fearless manner. These Souls can be natural leaders in that they are the first to take action. They do not wait for others, but instead take new directions without hesitation. Moon in Aries individuals can also inspire others to initiate their own life direction, and take action with bravery. In a negative expression, this can manifest as acting upon vengeance, and going on "the war path."

However, some may instinctively act upon fear, and recycle the past into the future. The Mars archetype can correlate with fear due to Mars being the lower octave of Pluto. This is due to the fear of abandonment, betrayal and loss symbolized by the Scorpio archetype. Of course fear can have many causes; the core point within this is that the need to move forward from the past must be embraced head-on instead of being met with fear.

In this situation, the need for forward motion, or continual momentum, is critical. This is because the new evolutionary cycle requires action. In so doing, the Soul can break past emotional patterns that are no longer supporting further growth. The transition from past to future will take place through the courage to initiate action, emotionally break from the past, and inwardly nurture the development of the independent voice.

The Moon in Aries individual will feel emotionally out of balance in environments that restrict independence and personal freedom. These Souls do not want to be restricted by anyone or anything in any way. In a distorted expression, this natal Moon can manifest as emotional dominance due to the emotional security that is derived from such behavior. This is because it creates a feeling of self-importance from an egocentric point of view.

These individuals can become insecure when somebody else attempts to assert their own voice and needs because it threatens the existing self-image and identity. In a natural expression, the Moon in Aries person will encourage and support others who seek to develop their voice, and become independent in their overall life. They will nurture themselves and others through cultivating an emotional space of autonomy, and the capacity to ask and answer one's own questions from within.

Aries as an archetype corresponds with our instincts. This is an essential point because instinctual emotional responses to the environment are emphasized here. For example, when the need for freedom is perceived as limited, or restricted in any way there can be an instinctual response of anger and frustration.

In a distorted expression, insecurity can lead to an emotional pattern of dominance over the environment. This is reflected in the natural square between the signs of Aries and Capricorn. The key here is to learn to respond to the environment instead of reacting instinctively. In so doing, fears of the past will be purged, and a new cycle is put into motion. Aries also makes a square to the sign of Cancer. This can manifest as the insecurity and fear of change which results in a recycling of old patterns into the future.

It is important to note that we all pick the environmental circumstances that we need in order to evolve. For instance, the Moon in Aries Soul may experience a childhood environment in which they must develop their own voice, and ask and answer their own questions from within in order to promote the necessary lessons and emotional changes discussed so far. A new emotional space and self-image free from the patterns and limitations of the past is then put into motion.

The need to trust one's instincts in the context of the new emotional patterns and self- identity is symbolized. The key within this is to nurture an emotional space of security to act upon the impulses that feel right, and not to act upon those that feel wrong on an instinctual level.

As an example, the Soul may create early childhood conditions wherein one or both parents wish to control the individual's time and/or put restrictions on their freedom, triggering the anger of Aries. The lesson within this is to minimize the reaction and develop a healthy response to the trigger. In these ways, the Soul can become self-secure, navigating the insecurity of the transition from past to future in order to embrace new beginnings. The emotional strength and spirit of the warrior can manifest, and become the underlying self-image within the Soul.

In order to evolve, the Moon in Aries person must embrace the opposite sign of Libra. In essence, this is to learn to listen and respond rather than react; in a reactive space, actions taken can lead to regret. This is reflected in the natural square to the sign of Capricorn. When the Soul is in a responsive space, it can become a true peace maker, and heal conflicts within relationships (polarity sign of Libra). For example, by learning to respond accordingly when anger is triggered, the art of diplomacy manifests.

The lesson is to cultivate an inner space of balance with respect to the need for freedom and independence by learning to listen to the needs of others. The individual can then better learn what to give and what not to give. In this way, they will come to find their own needs are met tenfold. By virtue of giving to others in this way, the Soul will then attract relationships that mirror this evolutionary intention of emotional balance and equality. Both partners will encourage and share an emotional space of mutual independence within relationships with equal giving and receiving. In an evolved expression, the dynamic tension between the past and future will be met with an uncommon fearlessness and strength to keep moving forwards no matter what challenges are faced.

Consensus State: In the Consensus State the Moon in Aries is expressed as a self-image and self-identity that is based upon the need for emotional development of the independent voice, and self-discovery within the mainstream society. The Soul will desire to progress within the social strata and will need emotional freedom and independence to generate whatever actions are deemed necessary in order for self-discovery to take place. The developing sense of identity is linked with advancement within society; to break into the new without restriction.

These individuals will have the capacity to pioneer or break new ground in whatever mainstream field of work they choose. This desire reflects the emotional need to be one's own boss, and to take the lead without waiting for others to act. This could then become a vehicle through which the individual gets ahead in the system. In a positive expression, the Soul will encourage others to grow by fostering the emotional courage to pursue new directions within the consensus. In this way, a sense of security is achieved, and a break from the past is achieved. The transition from the past to the future will then take place as these new emotional patterns are born. Conversely, the individual could act upon fears due to inner insecurity in such a way that the past is recycled into the future.

Individuated State: In the Individuated State this will manifest as a self-image and self-identity that is based upon the emotional development of the independent voice within an alternative field, and initiation of action that allows individuation to take place. The new, or unfolding self-image is rooted in self-discovery through individuation and breaking free from emotional patterns of social/cultural conditioning.

The Soul will desire to cultivate an inner space that feels secure to act upon the need to discover its identity outside the mainstream of society. The individual will require emotional freedom and independence to generate whatever experiences are deemed necessary in order for individuation to take hold. In this way, the courage to move forwards and discover a new dimension or aspect of themselves is accessed. Emotional security is internalized as the individual takes action upon what is unique and different for them and releases insecurities of the past linked with the need for self-discovery outside the mainstream.

Most commonly, these individuals will not tolerate any restriction of personal freedom to explore new fields that are outside the mainstream. This dynamic applies to gender assignment in the context of exploring new ways of being in relationships that do not conform to the accepted societal norms.

These Souls have the emotional strength and capacity to break new ground within an alternative field. In the best expression, they have the courage to break free from the consensus and can encourage others to do the same. The transition from the past to the future will then be made as the Soul develops an inner space of security with the growing need for self-discovery and is able to develop an independent voice within the alternative areas of society. The underlying emotional need is to embrace new directions linked with liberation from the mainstream without restriction, and in so doing break new ground.

Spiritual State: In the Spiritual State this will be expressed as a self-image that is based upon the emotional need to develop an independent voice through union with the Universal Source. As such, the Soul will require freedom and independence to generate whatever experiences are deemed necessary to spiritually progress. A new evolutionary cycle is linked with cultivating an emotional space that is rooted in the need for freedom to merge with God/dess in whatever ways are deemed necessary.

The key within this is that direct experience of universal, natural laws becomes a vehicle through which spiritualization takes place, and new emotional patterns are born. For example, the individual may initiate experiences of being alone in nature. Nature, and the natural laws therein, become the primary teacher, and a means for the individual to discover new emotional aspects of him or herself. The Soul will naturally seek to help others spiritually develop in this same way.

In essence, emotional security is internalized as the individual nurtures an inner space of courage which allows them to initiate whatever actions are deemed necessary to merge with God/dess; in so doing they release insecurities of the past which have prevented further growth. The Soul then gains the ability to break new ground through the knowledge of timeless, universal principles. For example, the individual could choose to teach these principles in a new way within a spiritual community that reflects the discovery/recovery of their own voice, and explores new directions with respect to spiritual growth.

In turn, the individual will encourage others to act upon the need to spiritualize in whatever ways they deem fit, and the courage to break from the emotional insecurities of the past linked with development of the independent voice. The transition from the past to the future takes hold as the Soul secures itself in the ways described above, and nurtures the need for independent spiritual progression.

**Famous people
with Moon in Aries:**

Bernie Sanders

Cate Blanchett

Virginia Wolfe

Mark Twain

Moon in Taurus: The Moon in Taurus symbolizes a self-image and emotional structure that is primarily rooted in the need to feel self-sufficient and self-reliant. In a positive expression of the Moon in Taurus these individuals will desire to secure themselves through a state of independence and possess the ability to look after and emotionally support themselves without the assistant of others.

Withdrawing into oneself to minimize the impact of the external environment creates emotional stability, and a feeling of self-preservation. An image that serves to illustrate the self-image of this natal Moon is the roots of a tree. This symbolizes the emotional need to "root" or ground into oneself. These Souls are inherent survivors. The evolutionary intent is to provide for oneself in any given situation and as such, these individuals have learned to become very resourceful. The key within this is that whatever has been identified for survival purposes will be linked with emotional security and stability.

Venus rules the signs of Taurus and Libra. Taurus corresponds with the inner side of Venus, our inner relationship with self. Libra symbolizes the external nature of Venus, our relationships with others. Our inner relationship is directly linked with our values and sense of overall meaning for the life. It also signifies our survival instinct. Within this is the procreative instinct, and the Soul's sexual values and inner orientation towards sexuality. As such, Moon in Taurus individuals will link their sexual life with their need for emotional security and stability. Sexual self-sufficiency is another important aspect of emotional security; to learn that their sexual needs are not dependent on a partner.

Commonly, the Taurus archetype manifests as the "frog in the well" syndrome. The small piece of the sky that the frog can see from the bottom of the well has become the total sky. For example, these Souls may work at the same job for a long period of time simply for reasons of financial security. The individual may identify a basic skill that can be used to sustain him or herself. This one skill then becomes the "total sky" so to speak. In this light, the inner relationship with self and self-image can become fixed and static. Taurus is a fixed, earth sign. This dynamic occurs because whatever the Soul has linked with survival will be highly valued. As a result, the self-image and resulting inner emotional patterns of the Soul can become "fixed" relative to what has been identified for survival purposes. Again, the key point is that emotional security is linked with these areas.

As mentioned previously, the need to withdraw from the impact of the external environment in order to consolidate is reflected by this natal Moon. Emotional stability is gained in this way because it is a means to facilitate internal security with one's inner resources and to nurture the need for self-sufficiency. As such, time alone or spent in isolation is commonly an essential emotional need for Moon in Taurus Souls.

The transition from the past to the future will take place through cultivating an emotional space of self-reliance and non-dependency. In essence, it is to nurture oneself via "doing for oneself" without relying on others. Emotional security will progressively shift from external to internal in these ways. For example, one possible expression this emotional shift can take is through making the effort to apply therapeutic tools to one's own situation in order to work through difficult experiences that are often linked with being thrown back on oneself without the assistance of others.

Many of these Souls have desired to essentially remain on their own because of an underlying emotional need to not be dependent on anyone or anything, and to nurture the need for self-reliance. Most often, in relationships these individuals will need to support and sustain themselves independent from the partner to feel emotionally secure.

Most often, individuals with Moon in Taurus create circumstances in their early life in which they are left to fend for themselves in various ways. These early childhood experiences serve to foster the necessary lessons of emotional self-reliance, self sufficiency, and independence. The dynamic of survival is emphasized.

For instance, the individual may have grown up in situations in which there were limited resources, or one or both parents were unable to support the child in some way. This triggers the emotional need to provide for oneself at an early age, and to secure oneself through the materialization of one's own resources. Another variation of this theme is to feel alienation and thus become isolated from the values promoted within the early childhood environment. In this situation, the Soul is thrown back on itself through such isolation. Positively responded to, this serves to root and ground the Soul into itself; the individual gains a sense of security through identifying their own values and resources without any outside assistance. It is important to note that these Souls will have an inbuilt resistance towards adopting the values of others that are incompatible with their own.

This type of early childhood environment has the effect of inducing an inner space of self-reliance in that most often the individual feels emotionally "on their own" due to the alienation and isolation that these conditions often create. The natural square from the sign of Aquarius to Taurus reflects liberation from outdated values and deconditioning of the inner relationship with the self. In some cases, depending on evolutionary state, this will manifest as individuation from mainstream values.

A central dynamic of this natal Moon placement is self-worth and self-value. As mentioned previously, the Taurus archetype reflects our inner relationship with the self, and the inner side of Venus. In a natural expression, Moon in Taurus people will nurture themselves through cultivating self-worth, and fostering a positive inner relationship. In essence, it is to learn that one's value is not dependent upon the value others give to them (inconjunct the sign of Libra). These Souls can have an innate ability to tune into the inner resources of others, and advocate making the necessary effort to actualize these resources. In this way, they nurture through encouraging others to be self-sufficient and energizing a similar emotional space for themselves.

As mentioned above, in a positive expression, these individuals will have an inherent ability to identify inner resources that can be utilized to effect self-reliance. This is reflected in the natural square from Leo to Taurus. The key within this is self-effort, and the ability to stand on one's own two feet. In so doing, the inner relationship with the self will change as the Soul learns to rely on itself, and creates an overall life style that reflects its own values. In a negative expression, the Soul will live vicariously through others, or vice versa. At worst, the individual will relate to others as personal possessions and objects because of the link to their own survival and thus emotional security.

In order to evolve, the Moon in Taurus individual must embrace the opposite sign of Scorpio. The sign of Scorpio corresponds with the entire field of psychology, and to understanding the "why" of anything. The Soul must transmute the limitations of mere survival via the courage to access deeper emotional waters. In the words of the renowned psychologist Carl Jung "As far as we can discern, the sole purpose of human existence is to kindle a light in the darkness of mere being." Scorpio reflects the natural principle of evolution, and the need to grow beyond areas of stagnation. The necessary evolution occurs through developing a psychological awareness of oneself, others, and life in general. The evolutionary need is to gain the psychological awareness of why the individual is emotionally put together or constructed in the ways that they are, and why others are put together in ways that they are. In so doing, the Soul will transmute the "frog in the well" syndrome that has been previously described, and grow to greater emotional depths and understanding. The Soul commonly creates situations of intense internal and external confrontation to facilitate this emotional shift. These confrontations have the effect of exposing pre-existing limitations, and evoking the need to release the security patterns of the past that are linked with survival. In so doing, the Soul progressively opens up to deeper emotional spaces.

Consensus State: In the Consensus State, the Moon in Taurus will manifest as a self-image and emotional structure that is founded upon the need to become self-sustaining within the mainstream society, and to emotionally support oneself via manifesting inner resources that can be used to advance within society. The individual's value system will reflect the values within the mainstream society of birth. For example, values that are commonly promoted in the West are social status and an emphasis on monetary wealth. The Soul will then relate through these values, and not relate to those who do not conform to the mainstream value system. Emotional security is linked with these values and inner orientation.

These Souls will have the capacity to sustain themselves through an inner resource or skill that is valued within the mainstream society, and to secure themselves through the actualization of these resources. This can then be used to nurture the need for self-sustainment, and effect progression within the social strata. This reflects the progressive shift from external to internal emotional security. However, in a distorted expression, some can adopt the attitude of making only minimal effort, just enough to get by.

Individuated State: In the Individuated State, the Moon in Taurus will manifest as a self-image and emotional structure that is based upon the need to decondition from the values of the mainstream society, and actualize inner resources to effect self-sustainment within an alternative field. The Soul must nurture the need for self-reliance through materializing unique resources and skills that reflects its individuality.

The individual will not relate to the prevailing mainstream values, and will desire to bond with others of like mind who share the same values. The individual will relate only to those who also seek to liberate from the values of the mainstream, and are learning to define their values from within. The key in this is to not become dependent on these bonds to feel inwardly valued, rather to energize an inner space of self-reliance from within oneself in the ways previously described. The inner orientation then becomes, if need be, to stand as a group of one.

In a positive expression, this Soul will secure itself by becoming self-sustaining via its unique gift(s) within an alternative field, cultivating an inner space of self-worth with respect to its individuality, and defining its value independent from the usual measurements of the mainstream. In the best expression, this will motivate others to do the same. The transition from past to future is made in this way. In essence, emotional security is internalized as the individual learns to value their individuality, stand as a group of one if need be, and actualize their unique resources outside of the mainstream.

Spiritual State: In the Spiritual State, the Moon in Taurus will manifest as a self-image and emotional structure that is based upon the need to become self-reliant through nurturing one's inner relationship the Source. Self-worth and value is linked with the relationship with the inner Godhead.

The Soul's inner emotional space is rooted in a primary relationship with the Universal Source, and through timeless, natural principles. Emotional security is progressively internalized via this primary relationship to God/dess. As a reflection of this, the Soul may relinquish all worldly possessions, and instead sustain oneself through accessing the inner wealth within. Only the Eternal can provide.

The key within this is that the individual must make the effort to actualize their inner resources that reflect the knowledge of universal, timeless principles in order to become self-sustaining. For example, the Soul could help others become self-reliant through encouraging them to cultivate a primary relationship with the Source, and become emotionally self-reliant and self-contained within external relationships in general.

**Famous people
with Moon in Taurus:**

Meryl Streep

Carl Jung

Bob Dylan

Pharrell Williams

Queen Elizabeth I of England

Moon in Gemini: The Moon in Gemini correlates with a self-image and emotional structure that is based upon the need for diversity. In a positive expression, this will manifest as an emotional space rooted in and expressing the natural principle of unity in diversity in some way. In other words, that there are many paths to truth.

This leads to the need for numerous experiences in which the individual is exposed to and can then collect a variety of facts, information and data from the external environment. Emotional security is linked with the intake of information and communication. These individuals are commonly very curious and have a strong intellectual capacity as a reflection of the need for mental expansion. These Souls are messengers.

Gemini is a mutable archetype which signifies adaptability to change. With the Moon in Gemini this manifests as the ability to adapt to many different environments. One possible expression is the ability to connect to many others through identifying a common thread that may be linked with a similar interest. Moon in Gemini Souls are highly relatable and others feel naturally drawn to open up to them because of this, seen in the trine to fellow air signs Libra and Aquarius.

The Gemini archetype corresponds with the left brain which is logical and empirical. Gemini symbolizes the component within consciousness that gives names and classifications to the physical environment, e.g, a chair, a cup, a table, etc. A logical and rational connection to the world is made through such classification. As such, there is commonly a natural need to secure oneself via the collection of information, facts, and viewpoints from the external environment. However, this can create a "revolving door of perspectives" in that the viewpoints and information are not assimilated in any cohesive way.

For example, the Soul may take in viewpoints from established authorities within any given field, yet these viewpoints may contradict each other. This triggers the evolutionary intention to discern the difference between opinion and fact, leading to the progressive feeling of security with one's personal truth: "what is true for me"? As the Soul begins to connect to the deeper truth, or root, of the collected information, it is then given a consistent reference point (Sagittarius polarity sign).

The Moon in Gemini Souls will most often process emotions through communication. The intent is to become secure enough to speak about emotional issues rather than just from the intellect. It is important to note that communication can take many forms. For example, a Soul with Moon in Gemini may feel driven to express themselves in verbal or non-verbal ways. They may choose to write, dance or paint.

The key is that they are able to move emotional energy by aligning with their most natural way of expressing themselves. The sign of Gemini corresponds with the hands, and many of these Souls express themselves through their hands. The lyrics from her song "Hands" by singer/songwriter Jewel who has the Moon in Gemini captures the emotional expression of this natal Moon: "These hands are small I know, but they are not yours, they are my own."

In a distorted expression, the Moon in Gemini manifests as both nervous talking and superficial communication, talking forever just to talk. This dynamic occurs because of an underlying emotional need to avoid or talk around the truth (polarity sign of Sagittarius). This can manifest as duplicity; a Dr. Jekyll and Mr. Hyde dynamic. The Soul fears that by facing and speaking the truth, rejection may occur. This is reflected in the square from Gemini to Virgo. Another expression this may take is the Soul being prone to gossip. The reason again being to avoid a feeling of insecurity by having to deal with their own emotional story.

Moon in Gemini individuals typically "intellectualize" emotions. In a natural expression, communication will occur only as necessary, and be centered within the emotional body. It is common for these Souls to align with work that involves communication of some nature such as writing, public speaking, and sales. Again, communication can take many forms and may also be expressed non-verbally. This dynamic occurs because these forms of work can serve to foster internal emotional stability.

The Moon in Gemini indicates a heightened sensitivity to words and verbal communication. This is because, in a positive expression, the individual can feel the emotions behind the words rather than just the words themselves. In a natural expression, these Souls can create an emotional space where others feel safe to talk and communicate in honest ways. The Soul allows for comfortable silences versus filling it with idle chatter. Silence is reflected in the square from Gemini to Pisces.

The nature of the communication within the early childhood environment is another crucial point to consider. For example, if the individual was encouraged at an early age to communicate as openly as possible, it will greatly impact the ability to communicate emotions in adult life. Conversely, if communication was not safe in early childhood then the individual is more likely to have difficulty expressing honest emotions in adult life. The key within this is to nurture the need for emotional expression and honest communication. The Soul will then nurture others in the same way.

In order to evolve, the individual must embrace the polarity sign of Sagittarius. The sign of Sagittarius symbolizes development of the intuition, alignment with natural law, elimination of delusive beliefs, and personal honesty. This means to emotionally center within the truth, or "root" of anything instead of becoming distracted within the leaves and branches. These Souls can then help others connect to the truth of any issue, become emotionally honest, and express themselves in very sincere ways.

In essence, the polarity sign of Sagittarius symbolizes the need to cultivate an inner space of honesty, sincerity, and to connect to one's personal emotional truth. One of the deepest lessons of this polarity sign is to become one's own inner teacher via intuitive development. The key within is that the intellect in and of itself does not know what is true and false; this is a function of the intuition.

Consensus State: In the Consensus State, the Moon in Gemini will manifest as a self-image and emotional structure that is based upon the need for diversity and the collection of a variety of information, facts, and view points from the mainstream society. It is important to note that the individual will feel insecure with viewpoints and information that fall outside the mainstream.

The Soul's emotional space is founded upon the need to gather a vast amount of information within the mainstream, and be shaped by the nature of the information that is absorbed within these environments. For example, the Soul may be attracted to busy environments because of the variety of experiences they offer. Progression within the social strata occurs through the intake of knowledge of how society is structured and operates within these different environments.

In a positive expression, an internalization and emotional assimilation of all the collected information will take place. In so doing, the Soul can emotionally center and secure itself within its own truth (polarity sign of Sagittarius). Emotional security is internalized via nurturing the need for expression of one's inner truth in a mainstream context. In natural expression, the individual will use the information gathered in such a way as to help others advance within the mainstream, and to express their personal truth through the knowledge gained within a diversity of environments. The shift from the past to the future will then follow.

Individuated State: In the Individuated State, the Moon in Gemini will manifest as a self-image that is based upon the need for diversity relative to the collection of information, facts and information outside the mainstream. As such, the individual may be attracted to explore many different alternative environments. Their emotional space is shaped by the alternative view points and information that depart from the socially accepted notions within the mainstream.

Emotional security is internalized as the Soul nurtures the need to express their unique personal truth outside the mainstream. For example, communication via writing, dancing, or art that reflects the Soul's individuality and personal truth can become a vehicle through which these Souls progressively become inwardly secure. The key within this is that assimilation of all the collected information allows emotional expression of their unique, personal truth within an alternative field or context (polarity sign of Sagittarius).

It is important to note that negative messages from those who felt threatened by these individuals may have been internalized (Moon in Gemini).

Examples of positive affirmations that can be used to effect emotional healing and inner security from such messages are: "I am just different, and my power lies within being different," and "if I need to stand as a group of one so be it." The transition from past to future will then follow.

Spiritual State: In the Spiritual State, the Moon in Gemini will manifest as a self-image that is based upon the collection of a diversity of viewpoints, information and data that reflects timeless, universal principles. The emotional space is shaped by this information and is stimulated by the need to explore many different spiritual environments.

The Soul may take in information and differing viewpoints from a variety of spiritual voices of authority as a reflection of the need for emotional expansion. Often these individuals will have a natural ability to communicate timeless, universal principles in a multitude of ways, like allegory and parable.

Information that is focused upon intuitive development and natural ways to know God/dess, such as different forms of meditation and connecting with a higher or eternal energy through the natural world, serves to expand one's understanding of spirituality itself. In essence, emotional security is internalized as the Soul roots or centers within its personal spiritual truth that reflects natural law. This gives rise to the ability to express the natural principle of the many paths leading to God/dess, or unity in diversity, in the way that feels most natural for the person. The transition from the past to the future is made via the assimilation of all the gathered information into a higher truth (polarity sign of Sagittarius).

**Famous people
with Moon in Gemini:**

Barack Obama

Jim Carrey

Tina Turner

Jennifer Lawrence

George Carlin

Moon in Cancer: The Moon in Cancer symbolizes a personal lens and self-image that is based on the need to emotionally nurture oneself and others, and to internalize emotional security. In a natural expression, the image of a universal mother, or mother to all, serves to illustrate this natal Moon. Positively expressed, these Souls are inherent nurturers. Most often, Moon in Cancer individuals are innately sensitive to the emotional states of others, and because of this, there is a cyclic need to return to the safety of the shell to emotionally stabilize. The ultimate intention for this archetype is learn to secure and nurture oneself internally by accessing the Mother within. Lahiri Mahasaya, who has this natal Moon placement, exemplifies this in his words: "Always remember that you belong to no one, and no one belongs to you."

This natal Moon placement emphasizes the impact of the early childhood environment. It is important to note that as children we take in our environment wholesale. A key evolutionary lesson of the Cancer Moon archetype is to learn the difference between the security of an external, and thus dependent nature, and internal security. In essence, it is to learn that the only true security that can be sought is found within by nurturing our connection to the Universal Source.

Typically, the mother or key female figure in early life plays a critical role relative to the dynamic of emotional nurturing. In a positive expression, the mother or key female figure will encourage the Moon in Cancer Soul to energize self-security and to self-nurture rather than depend on others for emotional security. This is reflected in the natural square between Cancer and Libra.

Conversely, the Moon in Cancer individual may pick an early childhood environment in which they are never really allowed to grow up. This may manifest as a mother or key female figure who emotionally suffocates the Soul. Overt or covert forms of emotional manipulation may also occur. For example, the mother may inject an icy silence whenever the Moon in Cancer individual attempts to mature and break away from an emotional dependency within the relationship. In a distorted expression, the Soul may then duplicate the behavior of the mother in adult life.

Cancer is a cardinal sign. The cardinal archetype is expressed as two steps forward, one step back. With the Moon in Cancer this manifests as taking one step out of one's shell, and then retreating back in again. This is due to a fear of vulnerability. In a natural expression, the Soul will self-nurture to embody greater levels of emotional security which minimizes emotional expectations upon others. These individuals will then encourage the same dynamic in others.

As security is progressively internalized, the self-image naturally changes to reflect this shift. In a distorted expression, this natal Moon will be expressed as emotional immaturity, and there will be a high degree of dependency upon external sources for emotional security. Again, this is reflected in the natural square between Libra and Cancer.

Commonly, Moon in Cancer individuals will create early childhood conditions in which one or both parents are emotionally unavailable and thus unable to meet their needs. This experience is intended to induce the necessary lessons of internalizing emotional security and minimizing any source of external dependency. Of course, as children we naturally expect our needs to be met. Again, we take in our environment without any filters. As a child we cannot understand why we are not nurtured in the ways we need, and as a result, displaced emotions are often carried into adult life. The key within this is to self-nurture and thus cultivate an emotional space of security for ourselves. In so doing, displaced emotions and dependences upon external sources to provide security are released. This reflects the transition from external to internal security, and how the Soul will navigate the transition from past to future.

The anima/animus dynamic is emphasized by this natal Moon placement. Over a great length of evolutionary time we must eventually integrate both the inner male and female. However, we incarnate preponderantly in one gender or the other. The Soul is naturally both male and female and simultaneously beyond gender (androgynous). As we evolve, the intention becomes to actualize both sides of gender equally.

As JWG teaches, a woman with an Aries Moon will not relate to the socially prescribed role of the stay-at-home wife. Similarly, a man with a Pisces Moon will not relate to the image of a macho man. It takes great courage and strength for men to show vulnerability in a culture which says men should not cry. Similarly, it takes the same kind of courage for a woman to take the lead in a society where women are expected to be subservient to men. In the highest expression, the Moon in Cancer manifests as self-security, and expresses both vulnerability and strength simultaneously (inner male/inner female). In essence, the Soul gains the internal security and strength to express the other side of gender.

From my view, one of the greatest teachings of the Cancer/Capricorn axis is that ultimate strength lies in being vulnerable; vulnerability does not equal weakness in this context. Strength comes from the courage to express pure emotion without fear.

In order for growth to proceed, the Moon in Cancer Soul must embrace the opposite sign of Capricorn. The sign of Capricorn corresponds with the need to establish a voice of authority within society, achieve emotional maturation, and develop self-determination. It is the evolution from the inner world to the outer world. The core point within this is that this sign reflects the need to accept responsibility for our own actions. An essential maturation then naturally takes hold.

A social role or career is a vehicle through which a personal voice of authority is most often expressed. Goals are then met through self-determination. As the Soul matures, external sources of emotional dependencies are released. The Soul will then encourage others to mature in this same way, and to establish their own role in the world. In the best expression, the individual will act as a supportive role model to others.

The Consensus State: In the Consensus State, this will manifest as personal lens and self-image that is founded upon the imprint of the early childhood environment. Typically, the biological family mirrors the cultural imprint reflected in the mainstream society of birth. This includes gender roles. All of these factors serve to shape and condition the self-image of the Soul, and are linked with emotional security.

For example, in most cases, women are expected to be the primary source of emotional nurturing in the family and home environment. Men are expected to be the primary source of discipline, and the bread winner.

The transition from the past to the future will take place through self-nurturing and creating an inner space of security independent from the family environment, to establish one's role in the world (Capricorn polarity sign). This allows progression within the social strata to occur. In so doing, emotional security shifts from external to internal sources, and the transition from past to future takes place.

The Individuated State: In the Individuated State, the Moon in Cancer will manifest as a personal lens and self-image that is based upon the need to foster emotional security through liberation from the mainstream. The intention is to embody self-security with one's individuality and individuation.

In this evolutionary state, the key is to embrace the growing feelings of alienation from the mainstream society, and to energize internal security with the unique self-image. This includes liberation from traditional gender roles. In so doing, external dependencies upon any social group(s) and the family environment will be purged. The individual will feel most drawn to nurture themselves and others through fostering inner security of their unique individuality. For example, the Soul may choose to work with alienated children or youths in some way. In turn, the individual will embody an energy that encourages others to become self-secure, independent of any social group and the family environment. In so doing, the Soul navigates the transition from past to future and emotional security progressively shifts from the external to the internal.

Spiritual State: In the Spiritual state, the Moon in Cancer will manifest as a personal lens and self-image that is based upon the need to embody greater levels of emotional security through union with the Source. An emotional space of self-security is cultivated through nurturing spiritual development, and a primary relationship with Source. The relationship with God/dess opens the emotional channel for the inner mother to be expressed. These Souls are inherently tuned into the emotional states of others.

In a positive expression an integration of the anima/animus will take hold. The Soul will progressively feel secure with both the masculine and the feminine in such a way that both are expressed equally. One way this may manifest is playing the role of mother and father simultaneously in some way. The Soul's "inner home" and personal lens will reflect the primary relationship with Source. The Soul will nurture itself and others through this relationship, and encourage others to energize inner emotional security through spiritual development. In essence, this individual will motivate others to return to their "root," or origins through union with God/dess. The evolutionary transition from past to future will then follow.

**Famous people
with Moon in Cancer:**

Kurt Cobain

Gwen Stefani

Jimi Hendrix

Courtney Love

Sean Penn

Moon in Leo: The Moon in Leo corresponds to a personal lens and self-image that is based upon a feeling of special destiny, and the emotional need for creative actualization; to take charge of the destiny through the strength of the will. The individual may be drawn to express themselves through music, acting or art; these Souls are intrinsic creators. In a natural expression, this manifests as the courage to follow the heart. The words of Rumi, who has the Moon in Leo, captures this emotional quality: "Why should I be unhappy? Every parcel of my being is in full bloom."

The sign of Leo makes us aware that we have something special to do in the world, inspiring us to manifest this unique gift or talent. The self-image is founded in the Soul's inbuilt abilities and feeling of a special destiny. The image of a flower blossoming serves to symbolize the emotional expression of this natal Moon. Moon in Leo people will feel most drawn to nurture themselves and others through self-expression; they are most commonly creative spirits, and have the ability to see the innate strength in others. Because of the underlying emotional need to take charge of one's destiny; these individuals are typically strong-willed. In a positive expression, the Soul will radiate a natural self-confidence.

The Soul may have created early childhood conditions in which one or both the parents attempted to direct the self-actualization process. In essence, one or both parents projected a subjective image on the individual, and then desired to shape their life path, or special destiny, according to this subjective lens. These conditions reflect the intention to take charge of the creative pull and manifest it through the strength of the will. In so doing, the Soul cultivates an inner space of security with respect to the need for self-actualization, and energizes self-empowerment instead of seeking security through external validation.

In a negative expression, this could be experienced as a very conditional love: "I will love you if and only if." The individual could then duplicate this behavior in adult life. In a natural expression, the parents nurture the individual via positive feedback in some way. This could come through the message that they are special, and reinforce the intention to self-validate instead of seeking the recognition of others. The Soul will then carry this lesson in adult life.

In a distorted expression, the Soul can become full of itself from an egocentric point of view. Most often, a pyramid reality structure is created in which the individual's needs are at the very top, and every other contributing life factor is expected to cater to those needs. This can manifest as delusions of grandeur; a *defacto* "king" or "queen" complex. Essentially the individual wants to be at center of everything in order to feel emotionally secure. Self empowerment can manifest via taking control of the special destiny through the strength of the will.

The sign of Leo correlates with the need for acknowledgment and feedback from the external environment. This dynamic is due to the insecurity of the preceding sign of Cancer. In a natural expression, the Soul will be secure with its inbuilt capacities and gifts, and use them to manifest their life's purpose. Conversely, some will actualize via delusions of grandeur because of an underlying emotional insecurity. The key within this is to internalize the need for validation. In this way, external dependencies upon the environment for recognition will be released.

In the very best expression, they will empower others to validate and actualize their own innate talents and potentials, and follow the call of their heart. The Soul will gain the ability to acknowledge the special gifts of others without feeling threatened. The true generosity of the Moon in Leo can then shine. This allows the evolutionary transition from past to future to occur as emotional security shifts from external to internal.

In order for evolution to proceed, the Soul must embrace the opposite sign, Aquarius. The sign of Aquarius corresponds with objectivity, emotional detachment, liberation, and deconditioning. It reflects the principle of like-mindedness. In essence, the intention is to link the special destiny and self-actualization with a socially relevant need. Liberation from the pyramid of reality will follow.

The words of Mahatma Gandhi, who shares this lunar signature, exemplify this ability to impact dramatic change with the magnitude of his heart: "You can shake the world in gentle ways." In a positive expression, the Soul will gain the ability to emotionally integrate as a member within a group or community instead of the need to be the star. Emotional detachment and disengagement from an overly subjective focus will create a necessary objectivity of how the Soul's intrinsic capacities can help society at large. Leo is ruled by the Sun. Just as the Sun provides life sustaining energy, so too does the light within these individuals have the potential for a far-reaching impact.

Consensus State: In the Consensus State, this will manifest as a personal lens and self-image that is based upon the emotional need to take control of the idea of a special destiny and self-actualize within the mainstream society. The feeling of a special destiny is linked with the materialization of creative talents and abilities which the Soul will desire to use to get ahead of the system. This is a vehicle through which the individual takes charge of their life purpose.

Most often, the Soul is dependent upon external feedback and validation from others within the mainstream to feel secure, and as that happens the individual becomes more empowered and self-sufficient. The transition from the past to the future will then follow. However, the Soul may choose to actualize in a way that reflects delusions of personal grandeur.

Individuated State: In the Individuated State, this will manifest as a personal lens and self-image that is based upon the need to take control of the creative purpose and destiny within an alternative field. The feeling of a special destiny is linked with the manifestation of intrinsic capacities that reflect the Soul's unique essence. In this evolutionary state, emotional self-empowerment will occur through liberation from the mainstream.

For example, the Soul could have a creative capacity such a musician, writer, or actor within an alternative group or community. This special gift then becomes a means to take charge of the personal destiny and cultivate a feeling of security outside of the mainstream. In the best expression, this has the effect of encouraging others to embrace their own inherent gifts which will in turn bring about emotional empowerment. In this way, the Soul can release the need for external validation, and the transition from the past to the future then takes place as emotional security progressively shifts from external to internal.

Spiritual State: In the Spiritual State, this will manifest as a personal lens and self-image that is based upon the need to take control of the special destiny, to become empowered, and self-actualize through union with the Source. The feeling of a special destiny is linked with the materialization of innate creative abilities that reflect the knowledge of natural, timeless laws. This becomes a means to nurture the need for self-empowerment and self-expression within a spiritual context.

In this evolutionary state, the individual emotionally relates to, or sees themselves as, a co-creator with God/dess, and acts as a channel through

**Famous people
with Moon in Leo:**

Julia Roberts

Mahatma Gandhi

David Bowie

Tom Hanks

Rumi

Paramahansa Yogananda

which the creative principle flows. Their inbuilt gifts will be used to serve the Source and so, by extension, others. These individuals may be seen in a special light by others relative to their knowledge of universal, natural principals. These Souls will encourage others to take charge of their destiny through merging with the Creator, and manifest the special abilities that reflect this union. The transition from the past to the future then follows.

Moon in Virgo: Moon in Virgo symbolizes a personal lens and self-image that is based on the need to be of service to the Whole, for self-purification, self- improvement, and to learn humility. These Souls are innate servers, and strive to make things better or right. Most often, service to the underdogs/under privileged is at the core of this natal Moon.

In the very best expression, this manifests as the ability to improve conditions and/or quality of life for oneself and others. For example, in my view, Robert Redford who has this lunar signature exemplifies this through his work as a conservationist and environmentalist. He has addressed pressing environmental issues in many documentaries for over 30 years.

In essence, it is through the sign of Virgo that we experience an inverted pyramid, and become aware of all our lacks and imperfections; of what we are not. The balloon of self-inflation reflected in the preceding sign of Leo is pierced. A good image would be of the proverbial spec of sand upon the beach. As such, a vibration of personal humility typically emanates the emotional body of those with this natal moon placement.

An emphasized focus upon our inner imperfections and deficiencies commonly occurs. This inner critical focus can be projected upon others and the external environment in general. The Soul will focus on what is missing or lacking with something versus what is working, hence these Souls tend to see the glass as half-empty rather than half-full.

In a distorted expression, this manifests as perpetual criticism and an overall negative attitude. Nothing is ever right or perfect enough. The psychology of victimization then takes hold. Conversely, the Soul can also become an inner perfectionist, always seeing a fault no matter how good the quality of their work. In this way, an inner space of emptiness and lack is created, and excessive crisis results.

These individuals may create an early childhood condition in which one or both parents are hypercritical. This has the effect of making the Soul feel rejected, reinforcing the inner focus and personal lens of lack, fault, and inadequacy. This experience is meant to induce lessons of creating an emotional space of self-improvement, self-adjustment, and healing, thus replacing emotional patterns of humiliation, rejection, and self-undermining behavior. The Soul can potentially become aware of the inner negative focus that is the cause of these conditions. In a natural expression, the Soul will pick a childhood environment wherein the parents foster an inner focus of self-improvement and the desire to be of service in some way; to shift the focus from what is lacking to self-adjustment as needed.

Virgo is a transitional archetype from subjective development to objective awareness. Aries to Leo symbolizes subjective focus and development. Libra to Pisces symbolizes objective focus and development. Any dynamic that is linked with the Aries-Leo orientation to life will feel "not right" or inadequate. As such, many of these individuals will feel a natural resonance with service and healing-oriented practices because they reflect the emotional shift described above.

All too often, a feeling of inner emptiness permeates the emotional body of the Moon in Virgo Soul. This creates a variety of avoidance or denial-oriented activities. For example, the "busy bee syndrome" commonly manifests. The individual is overly obligated to various external activities and never has the time to attend to their true and legitimate emotional needs. Denial of this behavior then results in the creation of rationalizations to defend it.

The Soul tends to identify only the apparent reality rather than the actual reality of any given situation. For instance, the apparent reality is never having enough time to do what the Soul knows it must do, resulting in the experience of constant crisis. The actual reality is the need to deny and avoid an emotional inner emptiness and void. The evolutionary intention is to fill the inner void through merging with an eternal energy, and aligning with one's right work.

The sign of Virgo correlates to the potential for sado-masochistic psychology and emotional patterns which has its roots in the myth of the Garden of Eden. In this myth, women are presented as the spiritual downfall of men. As a result, there is guilt linked with inferiority which creates the pathology of masochism and there is guilt linked with superiority which creates the psychology of sadism. Typically women manifest masochism, and men manifest sadism although the reverse can be true; they can also manifest simultaneously in the same individual.

As such, Moon in Virgo individuals will feel the need to adjust these dynamics from within their emotional body. As mentioned before, in a positive expression, self-improvement, making this "right," and service to the underdog are a central dynamic through which such emotional purification and egocentric humility will occur. This reflects the transition from the evolutionary past to the future.

In order for evolution to proceed, the individual must embrace the opposite sign, Pisces. The sign of Pisces symbolizes the need to merge with an Eternal energy, align with timeless, universal laws, cultivate a relationship with the Source, and to establish ultimate meaning from within via an overall spiritualization of the life in general.

It corresponds with the dynamic of completion and signifies that an entire evolutionary cycle is coming to culmination. In this way, the sense of inner emptiness and aloneness can be healed by inwardly merging with an eternal energy, the only place where true unconditional love can be accessed and found. Emotional patterns of victimization must be released as well. Self-compassion and forgiveness will replace the negative and critical self-image of the past. In the words of Yogananda, "Try to be a little better every day, and if you don't make it, just stand up and try again."

Consensus State: In the Consensus State, the Moon in Virgo will manifest as a personal lens and emotional structure that is based upon the need to serve the Whole, effect self-improvement and demonstrate personal humility within the mainstream society. In a natural expression, these Souls will have a natural ability to improve any work environment, and promote the attitude of making things better when possible instead of focusing on lack, fault, and deficiencies in general.

The individual will desire to get ahead of the system. Service to others within the mainstream can become a vehicle through which self-improvement and progression within the social strata takes place. For example, the individual could help others who are underprivileged to improve their life conditions in some way. In so doing, emotional security is progressively internalized as the need for self-adjustment and improvement is met from within instead of projected externally. The transition from past to future then follows.

Conversely, the individual may undermine this intention by focusing on themselves and others in a critical way, and sustaining the resulting emotional state of lack and inner emptiness. One way this manifests is in consistently pointing out the negative aspects of the overall environment in such a way that an inner space and vibration of victimization is maintained to effect emotional security.

Individuated State: In the Individuated State, the Moon in Virgo will manifest as a personal lens and emotional structure that is based upon the need to serve the Whole and for self-improvement within an alternative field. In this evolutionary state, the Soul will desire to self-perfect via liberation from mainstream forms of service, and actualize a specific form of work that reflects the Soul's unique individuality. However, the Soul may undermine or deny the need to individuate. Most often, this dynamic is due to prior experiences of rejection from others in the mainstream. Crisis will then take place in order to induce a necessary adjustment so that liberation from the emotional patterns of self-denial and undermining behavior can occur.

In the best expression, the Soul will naturally desire to serve others who have been similarly persecuted - the underdogs or downtrodden. Service to those who have been marginalized by those in the mainstream can become a means for individuation, emotional self-improvement and adjustment, and to actualize a form of work that reflects their unique form of contribution. In so doing, the emotional need for purification is internalized, and the resulting shift to self-security takes hold. The transition from the evolutionary past to future will then follow.

Spiritual State: In the Spiritual State, the Moon in Virgo will manifest as a personal lens and self-image that is based upon the need to serve the Whole, for self-improvement, and humility through union with the Source. The Soul's emotional space is rooted in the need to be of service to the Whole as directed by the Creator; in essence to help anyone who is in true and legitimate need in the context of one's "right work."

In this evolutionary state, the Soul will desire to serve others as a reflection of the desire to serve the Source. This becomes a means to create emotional self-improvement and adjustment and to fill the inner void of emptiness and aloneness. Typically, the individual will create excuses as to why he or she is not ready to perform the tasks as directed by a higher calling. The Soul becomes hung up on imperfections, lacks and doubts in such a way that it undermines the actualization of right work as directed by the God/dess, and reinforces the inner feeling of lack, fault, and imperfection. It is important to note that natural humility is an indication of true evolution. The enlightened masters of our time never felt worthy of the task. This is signified by the words of Jesus "Father, take this cup from me."

Service will revolve around helping others align with their right work, and self-improvement through merging with a higher calling. In this way, emotional wounds of the past that pertain to rejection, inferiority, and self-denial are healed. In so doing, the realization that perfection occurs one step at a time materializes. Healing centers and the use of specific meditation techniques are examples of service via spiritual development. Alignment with one's right work as directed by the Source reflects the shift from external to internal security as the releases emotional patterns of lack, doubt, and rejection. The transition from the past to the future then takes place.

**Famous people
with Moon in Virgo:**

Jodie Foster
Robert Redford
John Travolta
Eddie Vedder
Amy Adams

Moon in Libra: Moon in Libra reflects a personal lens and self-image that is based on the need for emotional balance, equality, role interchangeability and fair play. The emotional body is rooted in the need for giving, sharing, and inclusion, and to "do unto others as you would have done unto yourself."

These Souls are natural givers and highly sensitized to the emotional needs of others. The dynamic of listening is emphasized. The intention is to listen to the other from their reality in order to know what to give and what not to give. The image of a tuning fork serves to illustrate the need for equality and balance reflected in this natal Moon. These individuals are seeking to harmonize all discordant aspects within themselves. The words of Mahatma Gandhi capture this emotional expression: "Happiness is when what you think, what you say, and what you do are in harmony."

The sign of Libra symbolizes that an extreme as been reached, and that there is a need for returning to a greater state of emotional balance. The dynamic of justice and fair play is reflected here.

Libra corresponds to the initiation of relationships with others. It is through comparison and contrast that we learn about our own identity, who we are and are not. It signifies expectations and projected needs within relationships. It is through the initiation of relationships that we become aware of the diversity of individual needs, beliefs, values, etc.

Within this is the lesson about when to give and when not to give, who to give to and who not to, and when giving, what to give. By withholding giving in certain circumstances it can be an act of practicing a supreme form giving, by helping another to help themselves. This approach is advised when the same problem continues to be recycled within relationships and the Soul enables a dependency because of the perpetual need to give to others. A balanced state of equal giving and receiving can then be achieved.

Most often, this natal Moon indicates that emotional security is derived by meeting the emotional expectations and needs of others to the exclusion of their own. The core dynamic that creates this extremity is the need to be needed. Typically, Moon in Libra Souls operate through such emotional extremes. All too often, an imbalance occurs when the individual meets the emotional needs of others and in so doing loses touch with their own emotional needs and identity. Social withdrawal serves to help the Soul emotionally stabilize and get back in touch with its own needs. Again, the key is to balance the need to give with the need to nurture oneself; to nurture and give to the relationship and to oneself in a balanced and equal way.

Relative to the need to be needed, these Souls commonly attract partners who expect them to accommodate their reality in whatever ways that they wish. By giving to others in this way, the Moon in Libra individual feels needed and valued, and as if their own needs are also being met. Of course, this individual can manifest the opposite extreme, and/or the roles can interchange within the same relationship. This can be expressed as the counselor/counselee, student/teacher, dominant/subservient relationship type.

These Souls may create an early childhood environment which reflects these core dynamics. For example, one or both parents may have reinforced their own needs and expectations of who the individual should be. This is indicated in the square from Capricorn to Libra. This triggers the lesson to strike out on one's own outside of any relationship and to foster an independent voice (polarity sign of Aries). Positively expressed, a Moon in Libra Soul will have a parent who is also a natural giver, and energizes relationships of balanced giving and receiving, and reflect equality, and harmony.

At some point, if the Soul is over-giving to a fault, this situation of imbalance must be counteracted. The Soul can feel a progressive build up of anger because its own needs are not being meet, and this violates the need for equality, role interchangeability, and balance. This then necessitates that the individual assert their own needs and reality to their partner and others in general.

These Souls must nurture relationships only with others who have the ability to listen to reality as it exists for them and give according to that reality, and energize mutual independence within relationships. Most often, the partner will feel threatened or defensive when the individual asserts his or her needs within the relationship, and seeks to establish an overall equal reality. This is because the partner is invested in the Soul putting everything aside for them. However, when this shift is made the individual will no longer run the risk of losing him or herself to the needs of others, and can maintain a state of emotional balance and inner centeredness no matter the environment. Emotional security is progressively internalized as the Soul learns to balance the needs of relationships and their own needs instead of the extremes already described. The transition from the past to the future will then follow.

Evolution occurs for the Moon in Libra individuals through the opposite sign of Aries. Aries symbolizes the need for freedom and independence in order for self-discovery to occur. **The intention is for the Soul to take the lead in their own life.** In order to honor their own rhythm, these Souls must learn to listen first to their own instincts instead of always listening to the voices of others. In this way, the ability to ask and answer one's own questions is developed. This includes honoring their instincts as to when to be alone, and when to be with people. In so doing, true emotional balance can be achieved. A new cycle of evolution within relationships that is founded upon equality and mutual independence will then be put into motion.

Consensus State: In the Consensus State, this manifests as a personal lens and self-image that is based upon initiation of relationships with others within the mainstream, and conformity to the expectations of the status quo in society. The Soul will desire to get ahead of the system, and could initiate relationships with others in order to gain the necessary knowledge of how society is structured and operates for such progression to take hold. Emotional security is then linked with these relationships.

The need to collaborate with others is signified. We must all learn how to work as a team so that advancement within society can occur. In a natural expression, the individual will serve as a mentor to others, and advocate for justice, fair play and equality within the context of the mainstream society. The Soul nurtures itself in these ways.

The Moon in Libra Souls will typically be exposed to a diversity of social environments in which they learn of the varying expectations and needs within those environments. For instance, within the mainstream there are differing work places, social facilities, etc which have their own specific set of expectations, norms, and needs. This applies within personal relationships as well. The Soul develops an awareness of this dynamic through comparison and contrast within these differing social environments and relationships. Emotional security is progressively internalized as the Soul learns through such comparison and contrast which relationships and social contexts reflect their own needs and identity and which do not (polarity sign of Aries). The transition from the past to the future will follow.

Individuated State: In the Individuated State, this will manifest as a personal lens and self-image that is based upon the initiation of relationships with like-minded others within the alternative of society, and liberation from the expectations of the mainstream. Co-dependencies and imbalances within these relationships have commonly been created and have become a source of external emotional security.

In this evolutionary state, the Soul will desire to individuate through initiation of relationships that go outside the mainstream, as in non-conventional relationships in which roles are interchangeable, and are not dependent upon socially prescribed gender assignments.

Most often, the Soul has an emotional desire to share the need to individuate with the partner, establish coequality, and equal giving and receiving within relationships. These Souls will gain the awareness of the diversity of needs, values and beliefs of others in general. In essence, these Souls are learning to "hear" the individual needs of others. They will then determine which realities reflect their own needs and which do not.

The key within this is to act independently on the need for liberation rather than projecting it onto others within relationships, or waiting for others to act (Aries polarity sign). In this way, the Soul energizes an emotional space of balance and inner centeredness within any social interaction instead of deriving security through co-dependencies and emotional patterns of extremes within relationships. In so doing, the transition from the past to the future is made.

Spiritual State: In the Spiritual State, this will manifest as a personal lens and self-image that is based upon the initiation of relationships with others who also seek to spiritualize, and align with natural, timeless principles. Commonly, these relationships are imbalanced, mutually dependent, and are linked with external emotional security.

Within this comes exposure to a diversity of spiritual realities, needs, values, etc. Through comparison and contrast, the Soul then determines which realities reflect its own, and which do not. (Aries polarity sign). Alignment with timeless, universal principles will create emotional balance and equilibrium. The self-image is founded upon the natural law of giving, sharing, and inclusion.

In a natural expression, these individuals will encourage others to initiate relationships that are founded in mutual spiritual development. In essence, emotional security is internalized as the Soul learns to listen to its inner voice and instincts in regards to which spiritual path is best for them to follow instead of always listening to the voices of others. In so doing, the transition from the past to the future will take hold.

**Famous people
with Moon in Libra:**

Tori Amos
Claire Danes
Matthew Broderick
Loreena Mckennit
Julia Child

Moon in Scorpio: The Moon in Scorpio reflects a personal lens structure that is based on the need to penetrate to the core of its emotional body to facilitate growing past current limitations. The Soul will desire to emotionally penetrate and understand others in the very same way. In essence, this means that the individual will want to know why it is emotionally constructed in the way that it is, why others are constructed in the ways that are, and understand the underlying causes, or the "why?," of life in general. These Souls are innate psychologists.

Typically, they feel every emotion very intensely, and to its depth. The words of singer/songwriter Bjork who has this lunar signature captures its emotional expression: "I think every year brings unknowns that you have to deal with and handle, confront and embrace." An image of a deep sea diver serves to illustrate this natal Moon.

Unconsciously, these Souls may project the need for emotional penetration onto others, and others may project the same need onto the Moon in Scorpio individual.

Most often, these individuals have experienced an intense degree of emotional abandonment, betrayal, loss, and violations of trust. The intention is to learn who to trust and who not to. The dynamic of power/powerlessness is also symbolized. As a result, there is an emphasized sensitivity to this wound in others. This is linked with natural law of karma. We reap what we sow. It is important to note that karma can be 100% positive or 100% negative. It is one action leading to another action. These Souls are learning the proper and improper use of power.

Most commonly, the Scorpionic tendency is to try to conceal this wound from others and as a result can keep their emotional cards close to their chest. This can manifest as playing a more or less psychological role within relationships in which the Soul attempts to emotionally heal others with this same wound. However, the individual's true needs are not met as he or she also needs to heal wounds within an intimate relationship where total trust is essential. This can result in a re-creation of the wound if the partner leaves after their needs have been fulfilled by the Soul. Fear of commitment can result. A key lesson within this is to trust emotional body with respect to who has their best intentions at heart and who does not; who is trustworthy and who is not.

These Souls may choose an early childhood condition in which they experience loss, violations of trust, abandonment, and/or betrayal. For example, one parent could have left the scene which has the effect of making the individual feel abandoned. At worst, the individual may have been emotionally or physically abused in some way. In this situation, overt or covert forms of manipulation are used by those the Soul had trusted. This triggers the intention to learn who to trust and who not to, and purge emotional security patterns of the past that are thwarting further evolution. In a natural expression, the parents will encourage the individual to become aware of the nature of their limitations and the reasons, for these limitations. This cultivates emotional/psychological development and positive growth.

The sign of Scorpio reflects the need to metamorphose pre-existing limitations in order for continued growth and evolution to proceed. The need then becomes to intensely focus in on and inwardly analyze all current emotional patterns in order to understand the reason for those emotional patterns.

The core point is the Soul must confront and transmute habitual emotional patterns that are causing blocks and stagnation. Often, this is connected to external sources of power that the Soul has identified with for emotional security purposes. The need to emotionally detach from those dynamics then becomes crucial. In so doing, an emotional space of inner security is created in the context of nurturing one's inner power instead of relying on outside or external sources of power.

The psychology of cooperation and resistance is reflected here. Of course, we can choose to cooperate or resist the necessary growth and changes. In other words, we may choose to sustain the negative emotional patterns of the past. This is due to the emotional security linked with these patterns. In the very best expression, the Moon in Scorpio Soul will have the ability to uncover its deepest areas of resistance and limitations and grow beyond them. This can motivate others to do the same. At worst, this can manifest as compulsive manipulation or attempts to limit the growth of others in the overall environment. For instance, the Soul can manipulate others via the knowledge of their weakest emotional link.

Emotional patterns such as jealousy, possessiveness, and skepticism reflect the fear of having the emotional rug pulled out from beneath the feet. Such patterns create clear blocks from an evolutionary point of view. This emotional/psychological dynamic then creates the necessary confrontations to espouse it. The individual can then potentially grow to greater heights.

The sign of Scorpio symbolizes the need to emotionally unite with a higher source of power. This can manifest as an attraction to what are considered taboo areas of life such as the occult, divination, and/or sexual practices/rituals. The need to unite with a higher source or power reflects the emotional need for personal transformation and regeneration beyond current points of stagnation. These Souls may feel a natural attraction to these areas as they represent a source of emotional renewal and self-empowerment. In a natural expression, sexual rituals that are centered in the expansion of consciousness and union with God/dess are used to stimulate evolution. In a distorted expression, there is a compulsive focus on sexuality for profane purposes.

In order for evolution to proceed, the Moon in Scorpio person must embrace the opposite sign of Taurus, which correlates with the need for self-reliance, self-sustainment, and simplification. In essence, the Soul must look within itself to identify what inner resources can be used to energize an emotional space of self-sufficiency and independence.

Often, the individual is thrown back on their own resources in some way to induce the necessary changes. As the Soul extricates itself from external sources of power and emotional security, outdated emotional patterns of the past that are blocking further evolution are then eliminated. Emotional/psychological rebirth is felt as the Soul confronts and eliminates such patterns.

Consensus State: In the Consensus State, this will manifest as a self-lens and emotional structure that is based upon the need for transmutation, release of pre-existing limitations, and merging with sources of social power within the mainstream.

In this evolutionary state, the Soul will desire to get ahead of the system through aligning with sources of social power; for example, corporations, institutions, and organizations are all sources of social power that can be used to gain the psychological knowledge of how society operates. This knowledge can then be used to advance within society, so the Soul can move beyond the emotional blocks of the past.

In a natural expression, the Soul will use social power in a non-manipulative way, and confront others who misuse it. This reflects internalization of emotional security as the individual is seeking power from within itself rather than external sources (Taurus polarity sign). The transition from the past to the future then follows. Conversely, some individuals will use social power in a manipulative manner for egocentric purposes because of the emotional security it brings.

Individuated State: In the Individuated State, the Moon in Scorpio will manifest as a self-image and emotional structure that is based upon the emotional need for transmutation, purging of outdated patterns of the past, and merging with sources of power that are symbolic of the unique individuality.

In this evolutionary state, the Soul will desire to cultivate an inner space of self-security with respect to the need to liberate from the psychology of the mainstream. For example, astrology, past life regression, and Jungian psychology are all alternative fields that the Moon in Scorpio could potentially feel drawn towards to energize this emotional shift and growth. Attraction to the taboo is another area that can represent such transmutation as it reflects the unknown and a higher source of power.

These Souls will individuate through emotionally connecting with alternative psychological knowledge, and foster self-empowerment via breaking free from mainstream psychology. In the best expression, the Soul absorbs this knowledge within the emotional body in such a way that it can transmute habitual emotional patterns that are thwarting further growth. This can, in turn, motivate others do to the same. Emotional security progressively shifts from external to internal as the individual releases external sources of power and applies the knowledge gained in their own unique way (polarity sign of Taurus). The transition from the past to the evolutionary future will then take hold.

Spiritual State: In the Spiritual State, the Moon in Scorpio will manifest as a personal lens and self-image that is based upon the need for growth and emotional metamorphosis via elimination of areas of stagnation via union with the Creator. In this evolutionary state, the Soul will desire to psychologically re-empower and renew itself through merging with the God/dess.

Psychological knowledge of natural, timeless laws as reflected in the manifested Creation can be used to effect metamorphosis, and spiritually develop. This knowledge can be used to help others grow past emotional blocks and deepen their relationship with the Creator. The Soul will merge with others who also desire to develop in such a way that both individuals evolve out of past patterns that are inhibiting further growth, and emotionally commit to each other in the context of mutual spiritualization.

Emotional security is progressively internalized as the Soul purges external sources of power linked with spiritual teachers, communities, etc., and applies their knowledge of timeless, natural laws in such a way as to grow out of the limitations of the past and energize an inner space of independence (polarity sign of Taurus). Rituals that emphasize direct perception and emotional merging with the Universal Source are essential. The transition from the past to the future will then follow.

**Famous people
with Moon in Scorpio:**

Lady Gaga
Jennifer Lopez
Bjork
Ben Affleck

Moon in Sagittarius: Moon in Sagittarius reflects a personal lens and self-image structure that is rooted in the need to emotionally connect with one's personal truth for intuitive development, to release delusional beliefs, and become more honest. It symbolizes expansion as we embrace more and more of the total truth which is contained within the sign of Pisces. These Souls embody the spirit of the gypsy or nomad ever ready to explore new horizons. In the best expressions, they are natural teachers.

As such, these individuals will need emotional freedom and independence, as do all fire signs, to discover their personal truth. This is reflected in the natural trine from the fellow fire sign Aries to the sign of Sagittarius. Typically, these individuals will hold an inner space of emotional levity and lightness. They have a natural optimism which lends itself to a greater magnetism, and the capacity to see the light at the end of the tunnel; humor is often used as a vehicle for healing oneself and others.

The sign of Sagittarius corresponds to the need to understand life in a metaphysical, cosmological, or philosophical context, and to foster intuitive growth. Commonly, those with this natal Moon have an innate understanding that they are connected to something that is much larger than just themselves. It is as if the Soul intuitively feels there is a manifested creation, and that there are universal and natural laws that explain how creation operates. A core point within this is that belief determines how we will interpret life itself. There is a vast difference in a "belief" in something and actual knowledge which reflects natural laws. As such, the nature of the Soul's beliefs will become the basis, or foundation, of the emotional body, and linked with emotional security.

Some of these individuals will have a heightened emotional sensitivity to the natural universe. In these cases, Nature becomes a primary teacher, and the means to foster emotional security with one's inner personal truth. In the very best expression, this will manifest as the Daemon archetype. The Daemon Soul is highly tuned to the world of plants and animals and will feel more at home in this environment than anywhere else.

The Daemon Soul has the ability to fuse its consciousness with Nature in such a way that it becomes a messenger of the Creator. This quality is captured in the words of the well-known naturalist Jane Goodall, who said: "Chimpanzees, gorillas, and orangutans have been living for hundreds of thousands of years in the forest, living fantastic lives, never overpopulating, never destroying the forest. I would say that they have been in a way more successful than us as far as being in harmony with the environment." Her study of wild chimpanzees in Africa revolutionized the field of primatology.

The sign of Sagittarius reflects the intuitive component within consciousness. The intuition just knows what it knows without knowing how it knows it. A key lesson within this is to become one's own inner teacher. Typically, Souls with Moon in Sagittarius will manifest a very deep emotional wisdom that serves to trigger intuitive development in others. These individuals will have an innate ability to feel the underlying truth of any given circumstance.

Moon in Sagittarius Souls may have picked childhood environments in which one or both parents expected that they conform to the beliefs within the family environment. The Soul may have experienced restriction in the context of the need to discover its personal truth independent from the family environment. This has the effect of triggering the evolutionary intention to define truth from within oneself, and merge with natural Law. In a positive expression, the parents will encourage the individual to express and nurture the development of its personal truth even if it differs from their own. In essence, the guiding motto within the Soul becomes "our heart is our greatest teacher."

An inherent problem within this archetype is one of the generalization of truth. This describes a situation in which the Soul feels that their personal truth, whatever that may be, should be the truth for all. As a result, this can lead to a dynamic in which the individual attempts to convince and convert others to their personal truth, or truth as reflected by their specific philosophical or religious belief system.

The Soul will typically interpret others through the prism of its own emotional lens. All too often, they will attempt to persuade others due to an underlying insecurity. Emotional security is linked with their specific belief system. To have anybody threaten or disagree with these views or beliefs is to challenge the individual's overall sense of emotional security and stability. This then gives rise to the need to defend these beliefs to others.

Within this is the dynamic of honesty. The sign of Sagittarius corresponds to embellishments, exaggerations, and, at worst, outright lies. This is due to an emotional sense of inadequacy and lack. This is reflected by the square between Sagittarius and Virgo. With the Moon in Sagittarius this can be expressed as exaggerated emotional responses. The individual will overreact to the environment in some way and inflate their emotional state to others.

This sign also reflects the principle of continued growth and perpetual expansion. This natal Moon symbolizes an ongoing expansion of the Soul's consciousness and emotional body as the individual inwardly discovers and aligns with more of the total truth and natural laws. The difference between delusive beliefs and natural law, or truth, will then be felt, and insecurity linked with the need to defend one's personal truth to create emotional security is overcome. This is reflected in the square between Pisces and Sagittarius.

The need to discover or align with one's knowing of something must be met from within rather than through external sources such as an existing teacher, a religious organization, or philosophical system. In other words, the Moon in Sagittarius person must emotionally connect to their personal truth from within rather than searching externally in the various ways previously described.

The transition from the past to the future will take place through nurturing an inner space of security with the Soul's emotional truth and personal vision for their life. This is because it reflects the progressive shift of emotional security from external to internal sources. They can become natural teachers to others, and this has the effect of motivating them to develop their intuition. In addition, an emotional vibration of sincerity and honesty becomes the foundation of the emotional body.

These Souls must embrace the opposite sign of Gemini in order for evolution to proceed. This symbolizes the evolutionary intention to learn that, whatever the particular point of view, belief, or truth, it is relative, and not the only or absolute truth. In essence, the need is to learn that "truth" itself is relative. The natural law of unity in diversity is reflected in the polarity sign of Gemini. There are many paths that lead to the truth.

Once this lesson is learned, there will be no need to convince and convert others, and the individual will allow him or herself to be taught by others as well. This reflects that the Soul has become secure within itself in the context of its personal truth. This evolution commonly occurs through the intake of a diversity of information, ideas, and data from the external environment. Communication with others who hold equally as strong yet conflicting view points and beliefs as the Soul can evoke this critical lesson.

Consensus State: In the Consensus State, this will manifest as a personal lens and self-image that is based upon the mainstream beliefs of the society or culture of birth. The Soul's personal truth and resulting emotional space will reflect the mainstream beliefs of the society of birth. This lens becomes the prism through which the Soul interprets others and life in general, and is typically mirrored within the family environment. In other words, the early family environment and imprint has most often served to shape the individual's beliefs and personal truth in the context of the "truth" taught within the mainstream society of birth.

These individuals will only feel emotionally secure with others who hold socially accepted beliefs and viewpoints. In this evolutionary state, the individual will desire to advance within the social system. Higher education is a potential vehicle for such progression to occur. The key within this is that emotional security shifts from external to internal as the Soul aligns with its own personal truth within the mainstream environment.

For example, the individual may choose one particular religious organization over others as a reflection of his or her inner truth. Higher education in this specific field then becomes a means to advance within the social strata. The transition from the past to the future will then follow, and the Soul becomes internally secure enough to express its personal truth without the need to defend these viewpoints and beliefs to others.

Individuated State: In the Individuated State, this will manifest as a personal lens and emotional structure that is based upon the emotional need to decondition from truth as defined by the beliefs of the mainstream society.

As such, these Souls will need a high degree of freedom and independence to discover this truth from within themselves without restriction.

The intention is to create an emotional space that is shaped by a metaphysical or philosophical system that most intuitively resonates with the Soul. This system will be symbolic of the Soul's individuality, and reflect its inner unique personal truth. These Souls will need to discover on an emotional level what constitutes "truth." They will reject mainstream religious beliefs and assert the right for personal exploration of truth. In the best expression, this can motivate others to do the same.

Most commonly, alienation from country or society of birth is strongly felt. The Soul may seek out like-minded groups which share their feeling of alienation and the need to discover their personal truth. However, emotional security cannot only be sought through such like-minded others or groups.

The key within this is to emotionally expand via liberation from mainstream beliefs. This creates an emotional space of self-security to define truth from within oneself. This gives rise to the ability to communicate the natural truth that there is no one "right" way for all, and encourage others to also liberate themselves from mainstream truth and beliefs. The transition from the past to the future will then take place.

Spiritual State: In the Spiritual State, this will manifest as a personal lens and emotional structure that is rooted upon natural, universal laws. The self-image is rooted in these principles. Most commonly, these Souls will feel most at home within the context of nature and/or rural environments.

The intent is to become emotionally secure via actual knowledge of natural, timeless principles rather than rely on external teachers or spiritual communities. Many of these Souls are inherent teachers because of this knowledge and they will encourage others to become their own inner teacher through alignment with natural, universal laws. In essence, the Soul learns that only true knowledge of these principles creates true wisdom, not a belief in something. In essence, the guiding motto within the Soul becomes "our heart is our greatest teacher." This then becomes the foundation for emotional security. In so doing, the transition from the evolutionary past to the future takes hold.

**Famous people
with Moon in Sagittarius:**

Mozart
Albert Einstein
Adele
John Mayer
Jane Goodall

Moon in Capricorn: Moon in Capricorn reflects a personal lens and self-image that is rooted in the need to establish a voice of personal and responsible authority in society with maturity and authenticity. Emotionally speaking, these individuals will feel the weight of responsibility very acutely. They will have an emotional need to appear authoritative. Most often this manifests through a social role or career. These Souls are innate instructors.

Commonly, these individuals may have created experiences in which they were given many responsibilities and were forced to grow up fast. In some cases, this leads to a *defacto* parent dynamic in which they become the parent. As such, these Souls often feel older than their chronological age. The image of an adult within the child serves to illustrate the self-image of the Soul. In a positive expression, the parents will support the

Soul in nurturing their own voice of authority, to become responsible and self-motivated.

The sign of Capricorn symbolizes the need to learn how society is structured in order to integrate into the society. Any culture has accepted norms of behavior, and the expectation of conformity to these accepted norms, rules, and laws. Capricorn corresponds to the mainstream within any society. This sign signifies the psychology of reflection. In the best expression, these Souls will inherently reflect upon the various external factors in the environment that serve to condition, or imprint, the self-image and resulting emotional structure.

For example, the impact of the early childhood environment, the nature of the societal norms, rules, customs, and expectations, and influence of those in position(s) of authority both personally and socially are all external factors that serve to shape the Soul's personal lens. The need to manifest a personal voice of authority is most often met through an outer social role or career. This has the effect of cultivating emotional maturity and personal responsibility. The Moon in Capricorn Soul's sense of identity and emotional security is linked with their social position in society.

Typically, these individuals have come through a family environment in which they imprinted the overall structure of that environment; the "dos and don'ts", and generalized expected standard of conduct. The standard of right conduct is most often linked with the consensus or mainstream society of birth. This dynamic also applies to gender assignment in the context of the socially acceptable roles of men and women. The key point within this is that the Soul has emotionally imprinted these norms through the parental dynamic.

Capricorn reflects the issues of both guilt and judgment. Judgment is formed according to what we deem to be right or wrong, acceptable, unacceptable, etc. Such determination can be based on either the prevailing manmade, societal norms or natural law which reflects what is intrinsically right and wrong. There are two types of guilt. The first type is learned guilt, which is based on manmade morals, ethics, and norms. This must be purged from the Soul as it inhibits further growth. The second type is natural guilt, which is based on our own behavior and actions that are not in alignment with natural laws.

These Souls must reflect upon the causes of internalized guilt, both learned and natural. Natural guilt can become a means to learn from the mistakes of the past and make an inner determination to never repeat these mistakes again. The key point within this is that these individuals have most commonly internalized negative and false judgments from others when asking for their own emotional needs to be met. The expression of their own authority may have been negatively judged, or oppressed, by others. This reflects a source of learned guilt which must be released from the emotional body in order for positive evolution to continue.

Capricorn signifies the dynamic of control. These Souls may attempt to control others or the environment in general due to the emotional security that it brings. This is because control is a means to thwart or offset feelings of vulnerability. This creates an external appearance of being stoic, or always being in control of one's emotions. However, many of these Souls have a tender and sensitive emotional body. Deep inside there is an emotional *need* to lose control. This reflects the underlying desire to access vulnerability. This is reflected by the polarity sign of Cancer.

The lesson here is that ultimate strength lies in vulnerability. It is important to note that vulnerability is not a weakness, rather it can lend itself to the emotional strength to withstand the negative judgments of others. But above all else, when the walls of defense come down the Soul is better able to access the power of their own tenderness, allowing the Moon in Capricorn to tap into the eternal water element. It is within these waters that the unconditional love of self and others is accessed. This symbolizes that the Soul has become secure within itself, and emotional security has shifted from the external to the internal.

Commonly, in early life, one or both parents may have exerted an extremely authoritarian attitude towards the individual, and imposed a rigid standard of conduct. The Soul then internalized this imposed standard of conduct as correct. Deviating from these rigid standards creates an inner sense of guilt. In so doing, the Soul has repressed its own true and legitimate emotional needs via conformity to the expected norms enforced by the parents. These Souls have, in effect, learned to repress their own emotional needs in order to meet their existing obligations, duties and responsibilities. It is important to note that whatever becomes repressed becomes distorted.

This pattern is then typically carried into adult life. As a result, many of these individuals have displaced emotions that stem from the childhood environment in which their legitimate emotional needs were not met. The intention then becomes to allow the suppressed needs to surface in such a way that the Soul does not feel any guilt or negative judgment towards them.

Within this, accessing vulnerability in a safe and secure way is a key factor in energizing an inner sense of security and being able to release the patterns of emotional repression/suppression that are thwarting further growth. The individual must encourage him or herself to reflect upon the causes of this emotional displacement, and to accept the responsibility for these life conditions that are linked with the displacement. A natural maturation then follows. A healthy inner "adult child" is inwardly accessed as the Soul learns to nurture itself in these ways.

In essence, the Soul has become dependent on the various external sources described above for a feeling of personal authority, and as a means to judge appropriate behavior and conduct. The intention is to then become secure with one's internal judgment of what is right and wrong, acceptable and not acceptable, etc. Again, this is based upon what is intrinsically right and wrong as reflected by natural laws. The transition from the past to the future will materialize as the Soul progressively cultivates a personal voice of authority, breaks the pattern of emotional repression, accepts the responsibility in his or her own actions, and actualizes a social role that reflects the inherent capacities of the Soul.

In order for evolution to proceed, the Moon in Capricorn person must embrace the opposite sign of Cancer. The sign of Cancer reflects the need to become inwardly secure, to self-nurture, and to access the emotional body in a safe and secure way. We then learn the difference between security of an external and thus dependent nature and internal security. It is the evolution from the external to the internal world.

Authentic emotional expression will occur as the Soul becomes self-secure, accesses its vulnerability, and nurtures a personal voice of authority from within instead of depending on others in the external environment. The individual will develop an awareness of his or her emotional nature and self-image. The emotional body heals as the Soul breaks free from the emotional repression and learned guilt of the past. In its very best expression, this can motivate others to break free from the same emotional constraints and become authentic. In this way, these individuals can serve as positive role models to others.

Consensus State: In the Consensus State, this will manifest as a self-lens and emotional structure that is based upon cultivating a personal voice of authority within the mainstream society. The Soul will desire to get ahead of the system through the social role or career. This requires that they learn the rules, customs, and regulations within the mainstream of the society of birth. For example, to become a teacher or psychologist, etc., one must become certified. This requires that the individual learn the socially prescribed methods of doing so. The self-image within the Soul is shaped by these cultural norms, and societal rights and wrongs.

The Soul will conform to the socially accepted standards of behavior, including gender assignment, and emotionally judge itself and others according to these standards. In a natural expression, the individual will foster an inner space of security with his or her voice of authority to advance within the social strata, and use their social position in an ethical and responsible manner. They will hold others who misuse their authority responsible for their actions. As the Soul nurtures the need to manifest their voice of authority in society and matures in these ways, emotional security progressively shifts from external to internal. The transition from the past to the future then follows. Conversely, authority will be used in a manipulative way to realize personal ambitions and goals due to the emotional security it brings.

Individuated State: In the Individuated State, this will manifest as personal lens and emotional structure that is based upon the need to foster a personal voice of authority within an alternative field. The individual will desire to emotionally liberate from the socially accepted standards of behavior, and actualize a social role that reflects their individuality. The self-image within the Soul is shaped upon this individuation from the mainstream, materializing a personal voice of authority within an alternative field.

In a positive expression, internalized guilt that is linked with the need to individuate is purged from the Soul.

The key with this is that the individual begins to define what is right and wrong, what reality is and is not, from within. This includes gender assignment. The Soul will need to conform to the socially prescribed gender roles to create a sense of inner security, and desire self-authentic emotional expression. This can inspire others to do the same. As the Soul nurtures the need to develop its personal voice of authority outside the mainstream, emotional security is internalized. The transition from the past to the future then follows. Conversely, the Soul may repress the need to individuate, and create the appearance of normalcy due to the emotional security it brings.

Spiritual State: In the Spiritual State, this will manifest as a personal lens and emotional structure that is rooted in the need to establish a personal voice of authority through merging with the Creator, and within a spiritual community, group, or organization. The key within this is that the Soul must nurture the development of its inner authority via the relationship with God/dess, and not attach to any external role in a spiritual community from an egocentric point of view. In the same way, the individual cannot rely an external authority as a means to determine how best to develop spiritually, rather making this determination from within him or herself.

In the best expression, judgments will be based upon timeless, universal laws rather than socially prescribed rights and wrongs. These principles will also shape the individual's emotional space, and guide the expression of their outer role in the world. They will desire to help others develop spiritually through their social role as a reflection of the desire to serve the Source. This becomes a means to self-nurture, nurture others, and progressively shift emotional security from external to internal. The transition from past to future will then follow. They may be perceived as a spiritual voice of authority because of the knowledge of natural, timeless laws. In a negative expression, the Soul may attempt to secure itself through the voices of accepted spiritual authorities or an external role within a spiritual organization, community, etc.

**Famous people
with Moon in Capricorn:**

Brad Pitt

Johnny Depp

Reese Witherspoon

Kate Hudson

Moon in Aquarius: Moon in Aquarius reflects a personal lens and self-image that is founded on the need to liberate, individuate, and become emotionally objective via cultivation of an inner space of non-attachment. This sign rules the rebel, and their emotional instinct is non-conformity.

This sign most commonly feels that they are wired differently than most others so an inner rebellion can occur when they are placed in a conventional environment or forced to follow a mainstream model. They tend to be innovative and alternative in their thinking and can have a very fast working mind and nervous system. These Souls are catalysts.

As a result of feeling unique and different, they will want to connect with others of like mind as their unique vibratory nature may not allow them to feel as if they fit in, energizing a feeling as if they are always on the outskirts of society. In many cases, Souls with this natal Moon will forever be searching for 'their people' and these lost connections may seem hard to find. Once they do form bonds with others that feel to be 'cut from the same cloth,' they can often feel more like family than their own biological family. They can often be heard saying that their friends are their family.

Many of these individuals feel an emotional disconnection from the biological parents/family. It is like they are always on the outside looking in. The individual could have also experienced shock in the early childhood. The parents may have divorced, or been emotionally estranged in some way. This reflects the intention to liberate, decondition, and emotionally disengage. Positively expressed, the parents will encourage the actualization of the Soul's unique talents to validate their individuality.

This sign reflects the psychology of objectivity and emotional detachment. As a result, these Souls will typically appear unemotional and distant. It is as if they can never get out of their head. It also corresponds to trauma. Detachment and emotional disengagement from traumatic experiences leads to the necessary objectivity in regards to why the trauma occurred. In other words, detachment is often necessary for these individuals in order to process traumatic or cataclysmic events that may have occurred in recent lives as well as the current life.

Many people with this natal Moon placement are born with unresolved trauma. As a consequence, these Souls will need to cyclically disengage from the external environment, and from their emotional body. Disconnecting from their emotional body can serve as a survival mechanism in some cases for there can be emotional triggers that activate past life memories that are too much to integrate. As mentioned before, detachment allows the individual to liberate from the impact of unresolved trauma. As such, most often those with this natal Moon have an innate ability to stand outside of their own emotions and subjective experience. A natural objectivity then manifests. In its very best expression, this can have the effect of motivating others to heal from traumatic events through emotional liberation.

The sign of Aquarius corresponds to social groups and to the need to bond with like-minded others. JWG taught that there are three distinct social groups or movements that exist within any given society. The first sub group is the mainstream of the society which represents those who confirm to the consensus of that society. The second is the alternative or fringe group within society which exists apart or outside from the mainstream society. The third type is social dinosaurs which represent a group within society that advocate a vision of the cultural past should be the model for current times. An example of this dynamic that is currently occurring in the U.S is those that voice a desire to return to the times of racial, gender, and religious segregation of the past. The specific group that reflects like-mindedness is determined by the evolutionary state of the Soul.

Whatever like-minded social group the Soul has identified with has typically become a means for liberation to manifest. All too often, a dependency upon the group has been created, and resulting outdated emotional bonds and attachments are thwarting further evolution. The lesson within this is that the Soul must release these past emotional security patterns linked with social groups. In so doing, the individual will foster an inner space of security and gain the ability to stand as a group of one if necessary.

In essence, the intention is to nurture one's unique individuality from within, and a sense of security with the need to individuate will then follow. The transition from the past to the future will take place as the Soul embraces and opens up to its unique essence. For example, the Soul can "deprogram" the emotional body through the thought that their strength lies in being different. The individual will self-nurture and nurture others through the cultivation of their unique capacities. In these ways, emotional security shifts from external to internal.

The sign of Aquarius signifies rebellion. In order to liberate from the mainstream, the Soul must throw off and rebel against mainstream values, lifestyle, and expectations. While this is necessary, it can also lead to situations in which the Soul becomes emotionally secure via the act of rebellion itself. In other words, the Soul derives a sense of inner security by defining what it is against, or what it is not, without an awareness of what it stands for, or who the person is as an individual. Liberation then manifests as the Soul rebels, or rejects, the act of rebellion itself. An inner space of self-security is created through a progressive awareness of their own individual values, beliefs. In this way, the Soul energizes what it stands for, or inwardly values.

In order for evolution to proceed, the Moon in Aquarius Soul must embrace its opposite sign of Leo. The evolutionary intention is to take charge of their special sense of destiny, and to creatively actualize through the strength of the will. In essence, the polarity sign of Leo reflects the need to act upon the unique ideas and thoughts that serve to help society as a whole evolve without the support of a social group.

These Souls have intrinsic innovative capacities that must be materialized via the sign of Leo. They can then make manifest their innate abilities and talents instead of forever observing or sitting on the sidelines. The words of the late Diana, Princess of Wales, who has the natal Moon in this sign, exemplify this emotional growth: "I don't go by the rule book; I lead from the heart, not the head."

Consensus State: In the Consensus State, this will manifest as a personal lens and self-image that is based upon the need to liberate in the context of the mainstream environment, and bond with like-minded others. There are many different groups and subgroups within the consensus such as liberal, conservative, religious, etc. They will commonly feel as if they are wired differently from most others, although many will feel insecure with being different. This leads to suppression of the individuation impulse (preceding sign of Capricorn).

In this evolutionary state, the Soul will desire to progress within society. Typically, the individual forms bonds with others of like mind within the consensus community in order to gain the knowledge to get ahead within the social strata(s). In a natural expression, the individual will integrate within a like-minded mainstream community in such a way as to manifest their innovative abilities and advance within society. Emotional security is internalized as the Soul actualizes its unique and creative capacities within a mainstream environment independent from the support of a group or community. The transition from the past to the future then follows.

Individuated State: In the Individuated State, this will manifest as a personal lens and self-image that is based upon a growing feeling of alienation from the mainstream society, and the need to individuate to access its unique individuality. In this evolutionary state, the Soul will desire to connect with like-minded others who share the same emotional need liberate from the status quo. Most often, they will feel like a stranger in a strange land. These individuals may have experienced social isolation for not conforming to the mainstream.

Most often a dependency upon like-minded others and social group(s) is in place preventing further growth. Trauma can manifest to trigger the necessary severing of outdated emotional attachments. For example, many of these individuals have experienced social isolation for not conforming to the mainstream.

Liberation takes hold as the Soul inwardly nurtures the need to individuate and gains the ability to act alone when necessary; trauma from the past is then potentially healed. In the best expression, the Soul will integrate its unique gifts into society in such a way that it manifests its creative abilities in an alternative field (polarity sign of Leo).

The key within this is that such unique and creative abilities are materialized independent from the support of like-minded others and social groups or communities. This can inspire others do to the same. Emotional security progressively shifts from external to internal as the individual nurtures their individuality outside of any group or community, and actualizes their unique essence in the ways previously described. The transition from the past to the future will follow.

Spiritual State: In the Spiritual State, this will manifest as a personal lens and emotional structure that is based upon the need to emotionally liberate and individuate via union with God/dess, and alignment with timeless, universal laws as reflected in the manifested creation. In this evolutionary condition, the Soul will desire to form relationships with those who follow similar natural truths within spiritual organizations or communities. The common thread within such a community is the alignment with timeless, universal laws, and the desire to spiritualize.

Most commonly, the spiritual community has become an external source of security. The Soul must liberate from the emotional attachment to any group or friendship within the group, and decondition through a primary connection to the Source.

The intention is to materialize their special capacities without the assistance of the group. The Soul will then manifest a natural gift to help others break free from all sources of external emotional security and attachment through merging with God/dess. They offer innovative approaches to spirituality that reflect the intrinsic individuality of Soul. We all have a natural way to spiritualize that is in accordance with our inbuilt nature. In its very best expression, this can have the effect of motivating others to heal from traumatic events through the emotional vibration of transformation. The transition from the past to the future will then take place.

**Famous people
with Moon in Aquarius:**

Diana, Princess of Wales
John Lennon
Sandra Bullock
Neil Young

Moon in Pisces: Moon in Pisces reflects a personal lens and self-image that is founded on the need for ultimate meaning via a higher calling, to spiritualize the overall life through emotionally merging with God/dess, or an eternal energy, and for completion.

The sign of Pisces reflects the intention to embrace a transcendent reality that is rooted in universal, timeless principles that will be true regardless of the passage of time. These Souls are visionaries. The words of former first lady Michelle Obama who has this natal Moon capture this quality: "There are still many causes worth sacrificing for, so much history yet to be made."

This sign also corresponds to empathy, and high degree of emotional sensitivity to the overall environment. As such, these Souls will have a hyper-sensitive emotional body. In essence, these Souls absorb the environment wholesale, without any boundary or filter. As a result, at times, the individual will not be able to discern the emotions of others from their own.

It is important to note that the intention to emotionally connect with a timeless reality is typically not consciously known or realized. Until this intention is realized, the Soul will have a nebulous and unformed self-image and inner space. The Soul will commonly feel disillusioned with temporal values and belief systems in order to make this intention conscious. Feelings of meaningless and emptiness associated with temporal values and reality in general is meant to trigger the intention to merge the emotional body with the external, or universal source.

As JFG teaches, disillusionment is one of the most painful of all experiences, yet, in the end, it serves to align us with actual reality. The cycles of disillusionment will last until the individual makes a consistent effort to spiritualize their life, and embrace a higher calling. Psychic instability can manifest due to a loss of personal meaning.

These Souls may pick an early childhood condition in which one or both parents derive ultimate meaning from temporal values, and this then becomes their total reality. This can also manifest as various forms of escapism. For instance, one or both parents may use drugs or alcohol as a way to avoid an inner reality of meaninglessness and hopelessness. This leads to disillusionment, and facilitates the intention to create an inner space that is defined by what is timeless and infinite, and aligns with universal, natural laws.

In so doing the Soul is learning to foster ultimate meaning from within via merging with God/dess. In a positive expression, the Soul's parents will cultivate the development of inner meaning via encouraging a higher calling and/or a relationship with the Creator. The key point here is that meaning is defined from within instead of externally. As an example, the parents could give the message that the role itself, big or small, does not matter. What matters is the meaning that comes through the work performed.

Another variation of this theme is to create a life situation in which illusion becomes reality. This occurs when the individual has not yet realized the need to energize an emotional space that aligns with timeless, natural principles. The compensation for the inner emptiness and lack of meaning is to give temporal values and lifestyle ultimate meaning. In so doing, the Soul has created an illusionary image of itself in such a way that the illusion becomes reality. In essence, the individual avoids the meaninglessness associated with temporal values and reality through the creation of fantasies and illusions. At some point, the experience of disillusionment will serve to align the Soul with actual reality. The need to embrace spiritual values and a transcendent reality will then become deeply felt.

These individuals can also manifest a reality in which they feel much like an actor or actress in many different movies. Through the imagination the Soul can pretend or fantasize what it would be like to be this person or that person in such a way that they then create a false or illusionary personal lens or self-image that reflects the reality that the person symbolizes. Fantasy as reality is reflected in this dynamic as well. In essence, the individual can present the false image of themselves as real. This is due to the emotional need for escape.

In a distorted expression, this can materialize as deception. Of course, the Soul can also be deceived by others. It is important to note that there is natural innocence in these individuals that always wants to see the spirit of the potential in others. As a result, this often leads to a giant let-down when the other person is not able to or does not rise to the image that the Pisces Moon has envisioned.

Within this is the need to see others clearly. All too often, the Soul perceives reality through rose-tinted spectacles and does not see the actual reality of another person or situation in general; disillusionment then follows. What makes this very emotionally painful is that the individual cannot imagine doing to another what was done to them. Every time this is experienced it is like the first time. However, because of their forgiving nature they recreate this situation time and time again. For some Souls, the attitude then becomes "I can forgive but I cannot forget."

As mentioned above, commitment to a higher cause or purpose is a vehicle through which ultimate meaning can be established. Examples of higher purposes are non-profit organizations, charities, and a diversity of global causes. The Soul's higher calling becomes a means to unite with the Creator, and spiritually develop. This is because timeless, natural principles are expressed through the higher calling. Accessing eternal energy cultivates internal emotional security and stability. At its very best, this can inspire others to do the same, and align with a truly meaningful vision for the life.

In order for evolution to proceed, the Soul must embrace the opposite sign of Virgo. The essence of this lesson is to discern actual reality from illusion, one's own emotions from the emotions of others, and the difference between that which is finite and temporal in nature from that which is transcendent and universal. Right work can become a means to focus eternal energy. Proper priorities must be made. The intention is to only act upon the need for a higher meaning or purpose for the life, and in this way release illusions and delusions from the Soul.

Once the Soul makes a conscious effort to merge the emotional body with what is timeless and universal, they will no longer run the risk of creating false images that are based on fantasy or illusion. By cultivating a highly introspective focus based upon self-analysis, the difference between reality and illusion will be born out. The Soul will be able to discern its actual emotional reality verses the apparent reality. Meditation in one form or another is an excellent vehicle to make this emotional shift and evolution.

Consensus State: In the Consensus State, this will manifest as a personal lens and emotional structure that is based upon the need for ultimate meaning, and to embrace a higher calling within the mainstream of society. For instance, the Soul may align with religious organizations or humanitarian causes. Ultimate meaning is then derived from these sources.

In this evolutionary state, the individual desires to get ahead of the system through the dynamic of right work. In a natural expression, the Soul will commit to a higher cause or purpose within the mainstream in such a way that advancement will take place. In essence, the need for ultimate meaning is internalized as the Soul nurtures this need from within in such a way as to gain the ability to manifest right work within a mainstream context instead of the external sources mentioned previously (Virgo polarity sign). The transition from the past to the future will follow. In a distorted expression, the individual will live through temporal values often promoted within the mainstream, and resist the need to merge with a higher calling or purpose.

Individuated State: In the Individuated State, this will manifest as a personal lens and self-image that is based upon the need for ultimate meaning, and to emotionally connect with a higher purpose within the alternative field. In this evolutionary state, the Soul will desire to individuate through creating an emotional space that aligns with timeless, universal laws outside the mainstream. Most commonly, the Soul will experience disillusionment and a loss of meaning relative to temporal values reflected in the mainstream.

The intention is to cultivate ultimate meaning from within instead of externally in the ways previously described. In so doing, the individual can then materialize their right work in an alternative context (Virgo polarity sign). For example, alternative healing practices are possible expressions of a higher cause or purpose that reflects these principles and can becomes a means to merge the emotional body with the Eternal and to actualize right work. In the best expression, these individuals will have an innate ability to inspire others to discover their individuality through a higher calling. The transition from the evolutionary past to the evolutionary future will then take hold.

Spiritual State: In the Spiritual State, this will manifest as a personal lens and emotional structure that is based upon the need for ultimate meaning and to materialize a higher calling through union with the Creator. In this evolutionary state, the Soul will desire to spiritualize the emotional body through alignment with timeless, natural laws that are universally felt and experienced. The self-image and resulting inner space is then rooted in these universal principles, thus cultivating a relationship with God/dess.

Most commonly, ultimate meaning is projected externally onto a spiritual teacher, group, or community. Disillusionment is felt in the context of false teachings and teachers which do not reflect natural laws, and those who are not who they at first appear to be. The intention is to meet the need for ultimate meaning from within by inwardly nurturing the connection to external, and manifesting a higher purpose independent from any spiritual community, group, or teacher.

In so doing, the Soul will naturally inspire others to energize an emotional space that aligns with natural and timeless laws through merging with the God/dess. Right work that reflects this connection and is directed by the Source then materializes (Virgo polarity sign). The transition from the past to the future takes hold in this way.

In some cases, these individuals can impart a message that is received worldwide, and stands the test of time. The words of the great Master Yogananda illustrate this point: "Mankind is engaged in an eternal quest from that 'something else' that he hopes will bring him happiness, complete and unending. For those who have sought and found God the search is over. God is that something else."

**Famous People
with Moon in Pisces:**

Michael Jackson

Michelle Obama

Martin Luther King

Hillary Clinton

Chapter 2

The Lunar Nodes
by Sign and House

In this chapter we will discuss the core evolutionary intentions of the South and North Nodes of the Moon through the houses and signs from an evolutionary perspective relative to the evolutionary state of the Soul. As previously mentioned, the South Node corresponds with the prior life self-image/personal lens of the Soul, and its position by house and sign position signifies the dynamics of the past that represent conscious emotional security and familiarity. Most often, we will gravitate towards these areas because of the security that is linked with them. This creates clear limitations because of the habitual patterns that result from maintaining these emotional patterns. The North Node corresponds with the developing, or forming personal lens or emotional structure of the Soul. Its position by house and sign reflects the dynamics that represent the future and the pull away from the past.

It is important to note that these are generalized descriptions of the core intentions/meaning of the lunar nodes. Mitigating factors in the chart such as gender, cultural/religious conditioning/ and economic state will alter the expression of the core archetypes of the nodes, so we must analyze the nodal axis in the context of the evolutionary paradigm to arrive at an accurate understanding of them.

South Node in Aries/1st house, North Node in Libra/7th house

In order to discuss the generalized evolutionary intentions of the South Node in Aries/1st house and the North Node in Libra/7th house we must first review the signs of both Aries and Libra.

The sign of Aries reflects the beginning of a brand new evolutionary cycle. As such, it requires freedom and independence in order to discover what the new cycle is about. It is a masculine sign which corresponds to energy moving out from the center. It is a fire sign which signifies a sense of special destiny. It is a cardinal archetype which corresponds to the need to initiate change. Aries symbolizes self-discovery through initiation of action. Aries learns on an action/reaction basis. In other words, it is through reaction to a generated action that knowledge is gained. The analogy given to us by JWG to illustrate this point is a baby that touches a hot stove. The baby touches the stove and learns it is hot, the implied knowledge gained. It is through the initiation of actions that self-discovery occurs.

The sign of Aries signifies our instincts. For instance, we may be instinctively attracted to a new experience, person, opportunity, etc. Conversely, we may be instinctively repelled by any given life event. The key point is that by honoring our instincts in both situations, self-discovery occurs after the fact.

This sign connects to our fears. Fear can have many causes, and may lead to a resistance towards initiating or acting upon the necessary experiences that would lead to a new evolutionary cycle. Remember that a core intention of the sign of Aries is to break away from all that symbolizes the past so that a brand new beginning or evolutionary chapter can begin. If we make choices that are based on fear, and only act upon what is known and familiar, the past is then recycled into the future. Conversely, if we act to break free from our fear a new evolutionary cycle is put into motion. There is a natural inconjunct from Scorpio to Aries which reflects the fear of becoming overly embroiled in the needs of others, and the resulting restriction of personal freedom.

The nodal axis of Aries/1st house and Libra/7th house symbolizes an emotional paradox linked with relationships. On the one hand, there is a need for freedom and independence in order for self-discovery to occur (Aries/1st house), and on the other hand there is a need to complete the self through relationship (Libra/7th house). The intention is to balance the need for freedom and independence with the need for relationship. Within this, the lesson is to give to others first in order to have our own needs met tenfold. In essence, it is to learn not to create an either/or situation in regards to the need for personal freedom and to be in a relationship, rather to create a both/and situation in which both needs are meet.

The polarity sign of Aries is Libra. The sign of Libra corresponds to the need to complete oneself through relationships. In a broad sense, this sign signifies psychological extremities and imbalances and the need to balance such extremities. It represents an emergence into the social arena. In essence, we must learn to become equals with others, so the need to initiate relationships with a diversity of others is highlighted. Justice, fair play and equality are symbolized by this sign.

We learn who we are and who we are not through comparison and contrast with others within these relationships; which values, needs, and overall realities reflect our own and which do not. Imbalances and inequalities within relationships occur as soon as we lose touch with our own needs and identity. Co-dependencies arise due to the need to be needed.

It is in this way that we know how and what to give to others because we must identify reality as it exists for the other, and give according to that reality. A key within this is to learn when to give and when not to, and at times when appearing not to give it is actually practicing a supreme form of giving.

The extremes that can be played out within relationships are the subservient role and the dominant role. In the first extreme one partner is dominated by the other in such a way that they become a vicarious extension of the values, needs, and overall reality of the dominant partner. In this scenario, the individual will consistently meet the needs and accommodate the reality of the other to the exclusion of their own. In the opposite extreme, the individual will play the dominant role within the relationship. In this situation, they will expect their needs to constantly be met and that the other partner should accommodate their reality. The dominant partner may attempt to guide the development of the other partner's identity. These two roles can be fixed or alternated within the relationship. Again, the core dynamic that creates both of these imbalances is the need to be needed.

Now that we have discussed both the signs of Aries and Libra we can describe the generalized evolutionary intentions of the South Node in Aries/1st house and the North Node in Libra/7th house. What is the self-image and emotional structure of the past as symbolized by South Node in Aries/1st house? What specific dynamics constitute the Soul's conscious emotional security, relative to the past?

South Node in Aries/1st house

The South Node in Aries/1st house reflects that the self-image of the past is founded upon the need for freedom and independence in order for self-discovery and the development of one's independent voice to occur, and the ability to ask and answer one's own questions. There is a sense of special destiny linked with the new evolutionary cycle and with what is to come.

From a prior life point of view, the Soul has created a self-image that desired to remain essentially free from relationships in order to generate whatever experiences are necessary for self-discovery to occur. There is a feeling of special destiny and an emotional structure that is rooted in the need to break from the past so that a new cycle can begin, and to develop the courage to take the lead without waiting for others to act first.

Coming into the life, the Soul will naturally gravitate towards freedom and independence, and may be a natural loner. The instinct and emotional need to explore new life directions and experiences is emphasized, to feel life unfolding in such a way that self-discovery occurs on a daily basis. In a positive expression, these individuals embody the spirit of the warrior. There is an innate capacity to break new ground, in whatever area of life the Soul is drawn towards.

Most often, unresolved anger linked with restriction of personal freedom is carried over from the past into the current life. In an unevolved expression, the individual will not accept any restriction of action whatsoever, and will project the unresolved anger onto others. These individuals will derive emotional security from remaining essentially free and independent from any relationship so as not to become overly embroiled in the needs of others. In essence, the lesson is to balance the need for freedom and the need for relationship. In so doing, an overall reality of mutual independence is cultivated.

Consensus State: In the Consensus State, the South Node in Aries/1st house will manifest as a prior life emotional structure that is based upon the need to foster an independent voice within the mainstream society, and initiation of action in order to get ahead of the system.

In the past, there has been an emotional need for freedom and independence in order to learn how society is structured and how it operates, and the individual will naturally gravitate towards this on coming into the life. There is an instinctive desire to move forwards within the mainstream through learning the prevailing social norms, customs, laws, etc., that are carried over into the current life. In so doing, the Soul will progress through the social strata, and a new evolutionary cycle of will be put into motion.

The individual's sense of identity and self-discovery is linked with advancement within the mainstream society. These Souls will have the ability to break new ground in whatever field they choose, and can motivate others to do the same. However, some individuals may adopt a self-important attitude and attempt to dominate others within the social environment relative to the emotional security that it creates.

Individuated State: In the Individuated State, this will manifest as a prior life self-lens that is based upon cultivating an independent voice outside the mainstream of society. There is an instinct towards new experiences that allow the development of the individual to take place. In the past, there has been an emotional need for freedom and independence to act upon whatever experiences are deemed necessary to support liberation from the mainstream, and it is a natural point of gravitation coming into the current life.

In so doing, the individual is fostering the development of their independent voice outside the consensus. In the best expression, these Souls will encourage others to do what they must in order to similarly liberate, and in so doing "discover" themselves. However, some may thwart this growth by acting upon what is known and familiar and bringing the past into the future due to the emotional security that it brings.

Spiritual State: In the Spiritual State, this will manifest as a prior life self-image and emotional structure that is rooted in cultivating an independent voice through spiritual progression, and initiation of action to merge with the Source in whatever way the Soul feels most instinctually drawn towards.

Prior to the current life, the individual has learned to ask and answer their own questions through independent action upon the emotional need to unite with the Universal Source. There is an instinct towards new experiences that allows spiritual development and thus self-discovery to occur. In the past, the individual needed freedom and independence to spiritualize in whatever ways were deemed necessary, and they will gravitate towards this as a natural emotional need coming into the life.

A sense of special destiny is felt relative to a new evolutionary cycle that is based upon the need to rediscover or recover the independent voice via union with God/dess.

The Soul has acted to align with natural, timeless principles through independent experience of these principles prior to the current life. In other words, spiritualization has taken hold outside the influence of any spiritual community, group, or organization.

In this way the Soul has nurtured their own voice and gained knowledge of universal, timeless laws through their actual experience of these principles. In a positive expression, the Soul will use this knowledge to help others discover their own voice as a reflection of the desire to serve the Creator in some way.

North Node in Libra/7th house

What forming, or developing self-image and emotional structure will the Soul create in order to actualize the evolutionary intentions for the current life? What specific dynamics will represent the gravitational shift away from the past towards the future?

The North Node in Libra/7th house symbolizes that the forming self-image within the Soul will be founded upon integration as an equal with others, listening to the reality of others as it exists from them, and balancing the need for freedom with the need for relationship. In so doing, on overall reality of coequality is energized.

In essence, the key within this is to learn that the needs and realities of others are equal to one's own, and to give to others first rather than take. In this way, emotional balance and equality with others is fostered. The emotional paradox within relationships is resolved as the Soul initiates relationships with others that are founded on mutual independence and coequality. In other words, creating a "both/and" instead of an "either/or" environment in the context of balancing both the need for freedom and the desire for relationship.

As the life progresses, the Soul will feel the need to initiate relationships with others to evolve out of the emotional limitations of past, as reflected by the South Node in Aries/1st house. This shift away from the past is

77

reflected by the growing ability to listen to others in such a way as to then know what to give and what not to give. The capacity to use language that reflects the reality of the other and can be readily received develops as well. The underlying intention within is to learn how to deliver the message in such a way that it can be received by others.

The individual will progressively cultivate the inner security to support mutually independent self-actualization within relationships instead of remaining essentially free from others. A key within this is to create compromise as necessary, and to balance the individual's needs with the needs of the partner and others within relationships in general. In this way, the Soul will nurture an inner space of balance and equality with others. In the best cases, the Soul then becomes a natural giver.

Consensus State: In the Consensus State, this will manifest as a forming Personal lens and emotional structure that is based upon initiation of relationships with others in which they must work in a co-operative and coequal manner within the mainstream. In other words, the individual will necessarily learn to work together with others in order to get ahead within the system. For example, the Soul may create situations in which it must work collaboratively with others to achieve a common goal - as in, for example, to meet a company's needs or expectations.

The need to balance one's own needs and the needs of others relative to the desire to advance within society, and the needs of the partner, is essential. In so doing, mutual independence and coequality will be established within personal and social relationships within the mainstream society. In a natural expression, the Soul will develop the capacity to objectively understand the needs of others in order to help them progress within the social strata. The pull towards the evolutionary future will be felt as the need to integrate into the mainstream as an equal.

In a positive expression, the individual will also encourage others to work cooperatively with others, within both personal and social relationships. In a negative expression, the individual will create extremities instead of balance by attempting to dominate the environment, and by promoting competitiveness instead of cooperation. This is due to the emotional security that is derived from these emotional patterns linked with the past (South Node in Aries).

Individuated State: In the Individuated State, this will manifest as an evolving emotional structure that is based upon initiation of relationships with others who also desire to liberate from the mainstream. The Soul will desire to continue the process of individuation within the context of relationships.

The key here is to balance the need for independent actualization and liberation with the needs of the partner. In so doing, relationships in which both partners equally support the individuation of one another are established. The roles within relationships will be equal and interchangeable, and not defined by the expectations within the mainstream society.

The pull towards the future will be reflected by the need to balance the desire for freedom and independence from the mainstream and the needs of the partner. In so doing, the Soul will gain the ability to support others who also desire to individuate.

In essence, coequality is energized within relationships in which both partners independently act upon the need to individuate from the mainstream. In a negative expression, the individual will attempt to dominate the environment via asserting his or her need to individuate without truly listening to the reality of the other. This occurs because of emotional security that is derived from the emotional patterns of the past (South Node in Aries).

Spiritual State: In the Spiritual State, this will manifest as a forming self-image that is founded upon the initiation of relationships with others who also desire to merge with the Source. The Soul will cultivate emotional equilibrium through balancing the need for independent spiritual development with the desire to spiritualize within a relationship.

The lesson here is to share the knowledge of timeless, universal principles with others in some way, and within the context of relationship. In this way, the need to spiritualize can be met within a relationship. Both partners will mutually support the independent spiritual development of each other, and know how to give to another according to the reality of the other.

The individual will give to others in such a way as to help them also "give back" in the context of knowledge or universal, natural laws. Most often, the individual will learn to identify reality as it exists for almost anyone, and use language that reflects that reality. As such, natural counseling capacities can become a vehicle through which the Soul serves others as a reflection of the desire to serve God/dess. In so doing, the need for independent spiritual growth and the needs of others are balanced, and an overall reality of co-equality is nurtured. The ability to give back to others in a way that reflects the Soul's spiritual abilities then follows.

**Famous people with
South Node in Aries/1st house/
North Node in Libra/7th house:**

Michael Jackson

John Lennon

John Mayer

Kevin Spacey

South Node in Taurus/2nd house,
North Node in Scorpio/8th house

In order to discuss the core evolutionary intentions of the South Node in Taurus and the North Node in Scorpio we must first review the signs of both Taurus and Scorpio.

The sign of Taurus corresponds with self-reliance, self-sufficiency, and to the survival instinct in us all. This includes the sexual instinct, to procreate to ensure the survival of the species. It is through this sign that we identify inner resources that can be used to effect self-reliance and survival on an emotional and physical level. In essence, relative to the self-discovery reflected in the previous sign of Aries, we withdraw into the self to consolidate, or root, our identity from within.

This sign also symbolizes our values and sense of meaning within the overall life. Taurus, as an archetype, is feminine (energy moving towards the center), earth, and fixed (static). Venus rules both Taurus and Libra; Taurus corresponds with the inner side of Venus which is our inner relationship with our self, while Libra signifies the external nature of Venus which is our relationships with others. It is important to note that it is our inner relationship with our self, our inner vibration, that determines who we attract into our lives and the relationships we form with others.

The analogy that is given to us by JWG to illustrate this archetype is "the frog in the well." From the bottom of well the frog can only see a small piece of the sky, yet thinks this small piece of sky is the total universe. This creates clear limitations. Typically, this can create a "nuts and bolts" orientation to life in the sense of only focusing on what is needed for survival to be maintained. In a negative expression, the sign of Taurus can manifest as inertia or laziness. The key within this is self-effort in the context of actualization of inherent inner resources. Commonly, we are thrown back on ourselves in one way or another in order to induce the necessary self-reliance and the awareness of inner resources that can used to effect survival; to learn that we can "do for ourselves" so to speak.

The polarity sign of Taurus is Scorpio. The sign of Scorpio signifies the natural principle of evolution and it symbolizes the desire to merge with a higher source of power. Power can be used positively for self-empowerment and the empowerment of others, or negatively for egocentric and manipulative purposes. As such, learning the proper use of power is a critical lesson. It is through this sign that we become aware of our limitations, and learn how to metamorphose beyond those limitations. Psychological development is symbolized. The need to know how and why we operate the way we do and why others operate in the ways they do, is reflected by this archetype. By developing the psychological knowledge of why we are put together in the way we are, and the causes of our limitations, growth can occur; the frog is forced from the well.

The sign of Scorpio corresponds to the psychological dynamics of cooperation and resistance. We can cooperate with our current growth needs and purge past patterns of behavior that are inhibiting further evolution, or we can resist the necessary changes through maintaining these limited patterns due the security that is linked with these patterns. Fears of abandonment, betrayal and loss are symbolized by this sign. Fear of intimacy can result from these experiences. The need to learn who to trust and who not to is then critical.

Typically, the rug of emotional security is pulled out from underneath the feet to facilitate the necessary changes. In a natural expression, the individual will motivate others in a non-manipulative way to break free from the unnecessary limitations in their life, and to use themselves as the source of transmutation. In a negative expression, the individual will enforce a dependency upon him or herself as the means for change and evolution, and use this psychological knowledge in a manipulative manner.

Now that we have reviewed the archetypes of Taurus and Scorpio, we can discuss the core intentions of the South Node in Taurus/2nd house and the North Node in Scorpio/8th house. What is the emotional structure of the past reflected by the South Node in Taurus/2nd house? What specific dynamics represent the conscious emotional security of the past?

South Node in Taurus/2nd house

From a prior life perspective, the South Node in Taurus/2nd house symbolizes that the Soul has created a self-image that is based upon the need to become self-reliant and independent. A resulting need is to cyclically withdraw from the impact of the external environment, as it fosters emotional stability and renewal. It also serves to promote the identification of inner resources to effect survival. The individual will naturally gravitate towards these emotional patterns coming into the life. Whatever has been identified for survival will be highly valued.

Most commonly, the Soul has been thrown back on its own resources prior to the current life. In some cases, this creates a natural emotional space of self-reliance and independence. In essence, these individuals have been learning how to become self-sustaining, and to support themselves on the emotional and physical planes via their own efforts.

Coming into the life, the Soul will most often desire to withdraw from the impact of the external environment as it creates emotional stability and becomes a means for the Soul to root or ground into self. In so doing, the individual identifies their inner resources to support the underlying need for independence and self-containment. In the majority of cases, the frog-in-the-well orientation is created wherein the Soul has only identified a small, or isolated, part of the sky yet thinks this small piece is the total sky, so to speak.

This dynamic is based upon the survival instinct, and the need to secure oneself through whichever resource(s) have been linked with the ability to sustain oneself on an emotional and physical level. The inner relationship with self is then limited by this orientation..

In a natural expression, the Soul will highly value personal effort and self-sufficiency both in oneself and others. In a negative expression, only minimal effort will be put forward in regards to manifesting inner resources. In this situation, the individual will do just enough to get by. Most often, the individual will emotionally relate to others through the filter of his or her values, and be highly resistant towards others who attempt to impose their values. Of course, how this is expressed depends on the evolutionary state of the Soul.

Consensus State: In this evolutionary state, this will manifest as a prior life personal lens and emotional structure that is based upon the need to become self-reliant and independent within the mainstream society. The Soul will naturally desire to advance within the social strata via materialization of inner resources that allow such progression to take place.

Commonly, the individual is thrown back upon him or herself in some way. The purpose of this experience is to facilitate the necessary self-effort to manifest the Soul's inner resources to effect self-sufficiency within the mainstream. The individual will relate through the values of the mainstream and will most commonly derive emotional security from the accumulation of wealth and material possessions as they are linked with emotional and physical survival.

In a natural expression, the individual will highly value self-reliance and self-effort, and encourage others to do the same. The underlying need is to look after oneself without the assistance of others for such progression to take place. In a negative expression, the Soul will live vicariously through the values and resources of others within the mainstream, or attract a situation in which others desire to secure themselves in this same way through the individual. This dynamic exists due to the emotional security that it brings.

Individuated State: In this evolutionary state, the Soul has created a prior life self-image that is rooted in the need to liberate and individuate from the values and overall lifestyle reflected in the mainstream society.

Coming into the life, the Soul will desire to become self-sustaining and independent through materialization of inner resources that reflect the inherent individuality and unique abilities. In essence, meaning is defined through independence from mainstream society. The Soul will highly value the principle of individuation, and will seek to form bonds with others of like mind. The individual will only truly relate to others who also desire to individuate from the mainstream. The key within this is that a necessary effort must be made to do so; then the Soul will nurture the need for individuation from within itself instead of relying on others.

These Souls have typically experienced being thrown back on themselves in the context of the intention to decondition from the values of the mainstream, and to become independent from others to support the emotional need for liberation. For example, the individual may experience isolation from others within the mainstream society due to incompatible values.

Positively, this has the effect of turning the Soul in on itself in such a way that the individuation impulse is ignited. In other words, the dynamic of non-relatedness serves to trigger the necessary self reliance. The Soul cannot rely on, or live through, any group of like-minded others to materialize its inner capacities within an alternative field. The internal security to act alone if necessary is then energized. In the best expression, these individuals will consolidate by withdrawing into themselves so as to define their own values and resources outside the mainstream. In this way, the ability to become self-sustaining within an alternative field is cultivated.

Spiritual State: In the Spiritual State, the Soul has created a prior life emotional structure that is based upon the need to cultivate a primary relationship with the Source. This primary relationship is a vehicle through which self-sufficiency takes hold. Coming into the life, the individual will highly value spiritual development and union with God/dess, and universal, natural laws. This constitutes the core of their inner relationship. This then becomes the prism through which the Soul will relate to others.

Most often, prior to the current life, the Soul has experienced being thrown back on itself in regards to the need to spiritually develop independently from any spiritual community, or organization. In other words, the individual may have lived through the values of a spiritual community and created limitations from an evolutionary point of view. In this situation, the need becomes to align with universal, timeless laws in order to become self-sustaining outside of any spiritual group.

This gives rise to developing the inner resources to become independent and self-sustaining and so reflect the inner relationship with the Creator. In turn, the individual will encourage others to establish a primary relationship with the Source as a means to energize self-reliance.

North Node in Scorpio/8th house

What is the forming, or evolving, emotional structure of the Soul? What specific dynamics represent the pull away from the past towards the future?

The North Node in Scorpio/8th house symbolizes that the forming self-image is based upon the need to transmute limitations of the past that are inhibiting further evolution, and to develop a psychological understanding of oneself and life in general. In essence, to understand the "why" of things, and to merge with a higher source of power to cultivate personal growth and transmutation.

The sign of Scorpio evokes deeper levels of awareness. In this way, the frog will jump from the well and be exposed to more of the sky. As such, cycles of emotional/psychological death and re-birth reflect the pull towards the future; the desire to delve into deeper emotional waters.

Essentially, the Souls will learn to merge their resources and overall life in such a way that both individuals grow and evolve beyond what they were. The sign of Scorpio reflects the dynamic of commitment, and making a choice as to who to commit to and who not. Relative to the South Node in Taurus/2nd house, those who do not hold the same values as the individual will be excluded.

The individual will progressively gain the ability to identify the core cause(s), or the "why" of things instead of focusing only on the "how." In this way, necessary psychological knowledge is developed to grow beyond current limitations. Merging with a higher power propels evolution, and opens emotional channels to deeper levels of expression.

Consensus State: In the Consensus State, this will be expressed as a forming emotional structure that is based upon merging resources with others in the mainstream. Growth beyond the limitations of the past takes hold as the individual merges his or her resources with others in such a way that advancement within the social strata occurs.

The Soul will deepen its knowledge of how society works and operates through developing a psychological awareness of the central dynamics within the mainstream. For example, the individual may be exposed to those who hold more social power or knowledge than itself, and will desire to merge with them in order to acquire, or absorb, this knowledge. In so doing, an evolution beyond current emotional patterns that are creating limitations will occur. The pull towards the future will be symbolized by the need to unite existing resources with others in the mainstream in such a way that both partners grow past limitations.

In a distorted expression, the individual will attempt to manipulate others in the context of the desire to get ahead of the system and abuse social power due to the emotional security that it creates. The key point within this is that knowledge of how the system operates can be used to motivate others to advance, or used manipulatively for egocentric purposes. As the

Soul learns to commit to those who share the same values an evolution will occur; limitations of the past are transmuted through merging with others in a way to effect growth, to become bigger and brighter than before.

Individuated State: In the Individuated State, this will be expressed as a forming self-image that is founded on uniting with others in the alternative movement of society. Through aligning with those of like mind who feel similarly alienated from the mainstream society, a deepening of the Soul's inner resources and capacities occurs.

For example, the individual may progressively gain psychological knowledge of individuation through exploring the work of those who are well established in the alternative field such as Carl Jung, James Hilton, and Dane Rudhyar. Alternative psychological knowledge becomes a vehicle through which the Soul grows beyond its limitations. In other words, absorbing this type of information creates a metamorphosis as the Soul shifts from a limited understanding of "how" to a deeper understanding of the "why" of things.

An attraction to the taboo or occult may trigger the necessary growth and evolution. For instance, astrology, past life regression, and tarot are all possible fields that the Soul may desire to explore as they represent potential experiences of transmutation and personal growth. The pull towards the future will be felt as the need to emotionally and psychologically "deepen" through individuation from the mainstream.

Spiritual State: In the Spiritual State, this will be expressed as a forming self-image or personal lens that is based upon the desire to merge with the Universal Source to facilitate personal growth and evolution beyond current limitations. It is through union with God/dess that a deepening of the Soul's inner resources occurs.

For example, the individual may be attracted to rituals that promote spiritual development and growth such as Kriya Yoga. In this evolutionary state, the Soul can use the psychological knowledge of spiritual archetypes and timeless, natural principles to transmute emotional patterns of the past that are inhibiting further growth. This knowledge can be used to motivate others to evolve beyond their limitations, and to merge with the Source as a primary means to foster growth. In this way, a commitment to spiritual development is made. The pull towards the future is felt in these areas and a deepening of the Soul's existing inner resources in the ways previously described takes hold.

**Famous people with
South Node in Taurus/2nd house,
North Node in Scorpio/8th house:**

Ellen DeGeneres

Abraham Lincoln

Reese Witherspoon

Charles Darwin

South Node in Gemini/3rd house,
North Node in Sagittarius/9th house

In order to discuss the core evolutionary intentions of the South Node in Gemini/3rd house, and North Node in Sagittarius in the 9th house we must first review the signs of Gemini and Sagittarius.

The sign of Gemini corresponds to the need to collect facts, information, and data from the external environment. We must expand out into the external world relative to the self-consolation of the proceeding sign, Taurus. Such expansion takes place through the intake of a diversity of information, view points, and data from the external environment, through intellectual development. It symbolizes the left brain which is logical and rational, and deductive logic. Deductive logic attempts to build the whole from all the parts.

In and of itself, there is no limit to the amount of information that Gemini can absorb. This can create a revolving door of perspectives in which the point of view is always changing. The individual collects a never-ending amount of information yet it is not assimilated; the books go unread, and no interest is sustained within any field or subject. The core point within this is that the pre-existing intellectual structure will determine what information is considered valid and what is invalid.

The sign of Gemini corresponds to communication. In a negative expression, this will manifest as duplicity. In a natural expression, it will manifest as the ability to communicate information to a variety of people from many walks of life. The need to learn the difference between fact and opinion is symbolized. Mercury rules the signs of Gemini and Virgo. Gemini reflects the outer side of Mercury which is the collection of the facts, data and information in the external environment. Virgo reflects the inner side of Mercury which is the internal analysis and organization of the collected information.

The key within this is that the way in which we analyze and organize the information will determine how we communicate with others. For example, Mercury in Scorpio or the 8th house signifies that the Soul will naturally think in bottom line, psychological terms, and communicate with others in the same way. Typically, the individual will only talk when it is necessary. Mercury in Gemini or the 3rd house indicates a Soul that wants to take in as much information as possible, to experience diversity. The individual will most commonly talk just to talk.

The polarity sign of Gemini is Sagittarius. The sign of Sagittarius corresponds to the need to understand life in a metaphysical, philosophical, cosmological/religious context, and to align with one's personal truth. This then gives rise to belief systems of all sorts. Belief determines how we will interpret any given life event.

There is a vast difference between that which is based upon a delusive belief and that which is based on natural law and does not require a belief of any kind. I do not need a belief to know that the sky is blue, I simply know it is true. In this light, it is through the Sagittarius, 9th house, Jupiter archetype that we become aware that the truth inherently exists in and of itself and is not a product of the intellect or belief.

Natural laws are principles that are self-evident within the manifested Creation, and can be empirically validated. They are based upon direct knowledge gained through actual experience. This sign reflects the need to align with both personal truth and natural law, and eliminate delusive beliefs. It corresponds with the principle of perpetual expansion as the Soul embraces more and more of the total truth via the alignment with natural law.

The sign of Sagittarius symbolizes intuition, the component within consciousness that knows what it knows without necessarily knowing how it knows. It corresponds to the right brain which is conceptual, non-linear, and intuitive. It is the evolution from the part to the whole, to grasping the whole first and then allowing all the individual parts to fall into place.

Relative to the sign of Gemini, the intellect in and of itself does not know what is true and not true, this is a function of the intuition. Intuitive development will facilitate a shift from a potential "revolving door of perspectives" mental structure towards a consistent reference point for all the facts, information and data that is collected within the external environment to be interpreted.

An inherent problem of the sign of Sagittarius is that of generalization. Most often, the individual will generalize their personal truth and apply it to all. This can create the need to convince and convert others due to the emotional security that is linked to the personal beliefs. The dynamic of honesty is symbolized. In a natural expression, this will manifest as personal honesty and truth. In a distorted expression, this will manifest as exaggeration, embellishment, and outright lie(s). The reason for this is in an underlying sense of lack and inferiority which is reflected in the natural square to the sign of Virgo.

Now that we have reviewed the signs of Gemini and Sagittarius we can discuss the core evolutionary intentions of the South Node in Gemini/3rd house and the North Node in Sagittarius/9th house. What is the self-image structure of the past? What specific dynamics constitute conscious emotional security relative to the past?

South Node in Gemini/3rd house

The South Node in Gemini/3rd house symbolizes that the prior life emotional structure is based upon the need to collect a diversity of information from the external environment, and to communicate and take in knowledge with others to facilitate intellectual expansion.

There has been an emotional need to focus upon development of the intellect, and the rational, logical mind. Commonly, these Souls are highly curious and inquisitive and can be natural communicators. This will be a natural point of gravitation coming into the life, and represent the conscious emotional security patterns of the past.

The key point within this is that the nature of the information that has been collected is linked with emotional security. The Soul's pre-existing viewpoints, opinions, etc will determine what information is taken in and what is rejected. In other words, typically only information that supports a pre-existing viewpoint is taken in. This creates clear limitations. The Soul can become very intellectually defensive and reactive when its point of view is challenged. This dynamic occurs because of the emotional security that is derived from these view points. The lesson is to learn the difference between a reaction and a response.

In most cases, the individual will have a strong ability to communicate, and absorb a vast amount of information from the external environment. However, as mentioned previously, the information is not assimilated and there is commonly no sustained interest in one topic or subject. This creates the revolving door of perspectives in which there is no cohesive reference point for all the information that has been collected.

The Soul will be highly logical and intellectual coming into the life, and use an emphasized amount of mental energy. In a natural expression, these Souls will use the power of oratory to inspire others. In a distorted expression, this will manifest as duplicity. In essence, the prior life self-image and conscious emotional security patterns are rooted in the development of the intellect and the nature of the information collected from the external environment.

Consensus State: In the Consensus State, the South Node in Gemini/3rd house will be expressed as a prior life emotional structure and personal lens that is founded on the collection of facts, information and data within the mainstream society. Prior to the current life, the Soul has desired to get ahead of the system through collecting a wealth of information in regards to how society is structured and operates. The information that is collected in the external environment will be used to advance from a societal point of view.

Coming into the life, the Soul will naturally orient towards communicating and taking in information from others within the mainstream. When these view points are challenged the individual will typically become highly reactive and intellectually defensive because of the insecurity it creates.

In an evolved expression, information will be used to help others progress within the social strata, and to develop the necessary communication skills to share their knowledge with others within the mainstream. In this case, the Soul will have the ability to communicate with a diversity of others within the consensus. This reflects the pull towards the future. In a distorted expression, information will be used to reinforce subjective opinions and biases, and for duplicitous purposes.

Individuated State: In the Individuated State, the South Node in Gemini/3rd house will manifest as a prior life personal lens and emotional structure that is based upon the collection of facts, information, and data from the alternative movement within society. Prior to the current life, the Soul has desired to liberate and individuate from the mainstream society through the collection of facts, information, and data within alternative fields. Most often, the individual will be highly resistant towards the ideas, view points, and information in the mainstream.

Coming into the life, the Soul will orient towards communicating and taking in information for others in alternative fields. Commonly, the individual gathers information from a diversity of sources within a given alternative field in order to liberate themselves from the mainstream notions, view points, and practices within that field, thus serving to facilitate mental expansion and the individuation process.

Spiritual State: In the Spiritual State, the South Node in Gemini/3rd house is expressed as a prior life emotional structure that is based upon the collection of facts, information and data from spiritual communities, groups, or teachers.

Prior to the current life, the Soul desired to spiritually develop and merge with the Source through the intake of information founded upon timeless, universal principles. Information that is rooted in these principles will be the foundation of the prior life self-image, and the basis upon which the individual communicates with others.

This information represents emotional security in the context of the past, and can be a source of limitation in the current life. In a natural expression, this information can be used to communicate knowledge in a diversity of ways.

North Node in Sagittarius/9th house

What forming self-image will the Soul create signified by North Node in Sagittarius/9th house? Simply stated, it reflects the evolution from the intellect to the intuition, and from analyzing all the individual parts to first grasping the whole.

As previously mentioned, the intellect in and of itself does not know what is true and what is not, this is a function of the intuition. The Soul must learn that which is based on opinion (South Node in the 3rd house), and that which is based upon truth (North Node in the 9th house). As such, the pull towards the future will be felt as the need to develop the intuition and align with natural law and personal truth. Within this is the need to become one's own inner teacher.

The difference between a delusive belief and truth which reflects actual knowledge (natural law) will be learned through this emotional shift. In this way, alignment with one's personal truth will take hold. Delusive beliefs will be purged with the Soul. A balance between the left and right brain can take place (South Node in Gemini/3rd house, North Node in Sagittarius/9th house).

Consensus State: In the Consensus State, the North Node in Sagittarius/9th house will manifest as an evolving personal lens and emotional structure that is based upon the beliefs within the mainstream society or culture of birth. In essence, "truth" is defined by the beliefs and/or religion within the mainstream society of birth. The individual will then interpret others and life in general, relative to these beliefs.

The Soul will desire to get ahead of the system, and may use a credential in higher education (Sagittarius, 9th house, Jupiter archetype) as a means to progress within society. The specific beliefs or "truth" that the individual gravitates towards within the mainstream society will serve to create a consistent reference point for all the facts, information, and data in the external environment. These beliefs provide a means for intuitive development.

For example, by aligning with a specific religion that intuitively resonates with the individual and most closely reflects their personal truth, an assimilation of all the collected facts, information, and viewpoints takes place. This reflects the emotional shift towards the future. In a positive expression, this will manifest as an intuitive capacity to teach mainstream truth, beliefs, etc. In a negative expression, the individual will attempt to convince others due to the emotional security that is linked with delusive beliefs.

Individuated State: In the Individuated State, the North Node in Sagittarius/9th house will be expressed as a developing self-image that is based upon an alignment with personal truth independent from mainstream. The Soul will desire to liberate itself from the beliefs within the mainstream society and define "truth" from within itself.

Most commonly, the individual has collected a variety of information, viewpoints, and data from many different sources within the alternative movement of society. The current need and intention is to align with personal truth in such a way that it reflects the Soul's intrinsic individuality.

For example, picking a specific philosophical system that most intuitively resonates is a means of connecting with one's inner truth. In this way, a necessary filter is created through which all information is consistently referenced. Intuitive development can then follow.

There is an emotional need for freedom and independence in order to discover one's personal truth. Typically, the individual will resent any restriction of personal freedom to pursue their truth. In a positive expression, these Souls will encourage others to define the truth from within, free from the influence of the mainstream beliefs via their own example. In a negative expression, the Soul will attempt to convince and convert others to their individual personal truth due to the emotional security that is linked with these beliefs.

Spiritual State: In the Spiritual State, the North Node in Sagittarius/9th house will manifest through a forming emotional structure and self-image that is based upon an alignment with timeless, natural principles. Natural law will become the foundation of the developing personal lens. Intuitive development will then follow. In essence, the individual is learning to become their own teacher by uniting with Source, and universal, timeless laws. Natural law becomes the filter through which all the collected information is given a consistent reference point.

In this evolutionary state, the Soul will most commonly advocate direct experience of natural law as a means to develop spiritually. Nature, and the natural laws therein, can become a primary teacher. In a positive expression the individual gains the ability to teach the principles to others, and promote intuitive development as a means to connect to the Creator. This symbolizes the emotional shift towards the future.

**Famous people with
South Node in Gemini/3rd house/
North Node in Sagittarius/9th house:**

Angelina Jolie

Leonardo Dicaprio

Jewel

Tom Hanks

South Node in Cancer/4th house,
North Node in Capricorn/10th house

In order to discuss the core intentions of the South Node in Cancer/4th house and the North Node in Capricorn/10th house we must review the signs of Cancer and Capricorn.

The sign of Cancer symbolizes the emotional structure and self-image of the Soul. Following the sign of Gemini, we form a personal relationship with all the information we have collected which then generates a distinct self-image or personal lens.

The sign of Cancer corresponds with the early childhood environment. As children we have no defenses, and take in our environment wholesale. It most commonly symbolizes the mother, key female figure, or the parent who played the primary nurturing role. This sign highlights the dynamic of nurturing.

As children, we naturally expect to have our emotional needs met by our parents. Typically, when these needs go unfilled, displaced emotions are carried over into adult life. One of the deepest lessons of this sign is to learn the difference between security of an external, and thus dependent, nature, and security of an internal nature which is non-dependent. We must minimize our expectations upon others to meet our emotional security needs. Commonly, external sources of emotional security are removed in one way or another to trigger the lessons of self-security.

The anima/animus dynamic is signified by this sign. Over a great length of evolutionary time an integration of the inner male/inner female occurs. The Soul is simultaneously male and female and beyond gender, although it incarnates preponderantly in one gender or the other. Through an integration of both the masculine and the feminine a state of androgyny is reached. Progressively, we become secure with both the masculine and feminine principles within ourselves, and then gain the ability to express them equally in a way that is independent from the socially prescribed gender roles. Gender assignment is reflected by the polarity sign of Capricorn.

For example, in a natural expression a man with a Pisces Moon will feel inwardly secure enough to show his natural vulnerability and sensitivity, and not need to compensate by taking on the persona of a macho man. Similarly, a woman with an Aries Moon will feel secure to initiate whatever life path or direction she feels instinctively drawn towards, to walk as an equal with a man even if it does not conform to the socially accepted roles for women.

The sign of Capricorn symbolizes the societal norms, rules, traditions and customs within a culture or nation, in the mainstream of society. Every nation or culture has rules, taboos, and "rights and wrongs" to which we are expected to conform. Gender assignment is an aspect of social norms within the mainstream. These social norms then serve as conditioning factors within consciousness.

The sign of Capricorn reflects the structure of consciousness. It corresponds to the need to learn how society is structured and operates to advance within the social strata. It reflects the need to establish a personal voice of authority within society. The social role, or career, most often becomes a vehicle through which that voice is developed.

The sign of Capricorn symbolizes the dynamic of guilt. There are two types of guilt. The first type is learned guilt which is based on man-made laws. This type of guilt must be jettisoned from the Soul as it inhibits further growth. The second type is natural guilt, which is based upon any action that violates natural law. This type of guilt serves to teach the Soul to never act in the same way again. Repression and suppression of emotion can occur because of an accumulation of learned guilt. Whatever becomes repressed becomes distorted.

Emotional maturation is developed through accepting the responsibility for our own actions. Reflection is an important aspect of this sign. Reflection induces the necessary awareness of what has become crystallized, outdated within ourselves, and is preventing further growth. In so doing, we can then restructure in a positive way that facilitates emotional maturation, cultivation of a personal voice of authority, and authenticity.

Now that we have reviewed the signs of Cancer and Capricorn, we can discuss the core intentions of the South Node in Cancer/4th house and the North Node in Capricorn/10th house. What was the emotional structure and personal lens of the past? What specific dynamics represent the conscious emotional security patterns of the past?

The South Node in Cancer/4th house

The South Node in Cancer/4th house symbolizes that the prior life emotional structure is based upon the need to internalize emotional security, self-nurture, and highlights the impact of the early childhood environment. Dependencies upon the external environment linked with emotional security are a source of limitation and stagnation relative to the past.

Coming into the life, the Soul will gravitate to these same dynamics. These individuals will experience the removal of all types of sources of external security. These experiences are meant to trigger the emotional shift from external to internal security; to nurture an inner space of self-security.

Typically, one or both parents are unable to fulfill the Soul's emotional needs. This has the effect of throwing the Soul back in on itself to minimize external dependencies and cultivate an emotional space of internal security.

In some cases, the Soul may come into adult life with displaced emotions intact, and expect others to fulfill these childhood needs. In so doing, a *defacto* parental dynamic is created within relationships. In other cases, the individual may choose to nurture others as a vicarious way of healing childhood wounds. The key within this is that self-nurturing provides a means to foster inner security. Emotional security is then internalized, and childhood wounds can truly heal. These individuals may attract others who are, or appear to be, just as needy as themselves as a compensation for their own insecurity. These dynamics reflect a limitation of the past that is preventing further growth.

Consensus State: In the Consensus State, the South Node in Cancer/4th house will manifest as a prior emotional structure and personal lens that is based upon the overall imprint within the family and mainstream environment. For example, the Soul internalizes the role of male/female through the biological mother and father in early life. The individual most often derives emotional security through the early childhood imprint of these socially accepted roles and gender assignments.

The individual will desire to get ahead within the system and typically gravitate to the imprint within the family environment in order to advance within society. In other words, the Soul conforms to the ways that the parents integrated within society in early childhood. In a positive expression, the Soul can use the imprint in the early childhood environment to foster internal security and to self-nurture. In a negative expression, the individual will sustain emotional dependencies of the past linked with the family of birth due to the security linked with these patterns.

Individuated State: In the Individuated State, the South Node in Cancer/4th house will manifest as a prior life self-image that is based upon feeling different than those in the mainstream of society, and the need to individuate. Yet, the need to individuate often creates insecurity. Commonly, the Soul has created close bonds with others of like mind prior to the current life. These bonds have had the effect of shaping the self-image, and are linked with emotional security.

The intention is to cultivate internal security with the need for individuation, and liberate from any dependency upon a social group or the family environment to nurture their individuality. In this way, the Soul energizes an inner space of self-security independent from the influence of like-minded others. The individual will not relate to the traditional roles within relationships reflected in the mainstream society.

The individual will rebel, or reject, the socially prescribed gender assignments, which may cause an emotional detachment from the family environment if socially accepted roles within the mainstream are reinforced. The key within this is that the Soul is learning to nurture its individuality from within instead of through external sources. In so doing, the ability to stand alone if necessary is gained, and an emotional space of security is fostered. Conversely, the individual derives emotional security through a social group and/or family environment.

Spiritual State: In the Spiritual State, the South Node in Cancer/4th house will manifest as a prior life emotional structure that is based upon the desire to merge and unite with the Source as a primary means of self-security. We can cultivate an "inner home," so to speak, within ourselves through this union.

Typically, close bonds were formed with those who also seek to develop spiritually prior to the current life. These bonds have had a significant impact upon the self-image. Emotional dependencies upon these relationships then create limitations in the context of further growth.

In this evolutionary state, timeless, natural principles are the foundation of the self-image. The anima/animus is integrated through union with God/dess in such a way that the Soul can equally express both the masculine and feminine principles. For example, the individual can play the role of the mother and father simultaneously. These Souls then encourage others to self-nurture and foster self-security via a primary relationship with the Universal Source.

North Node in Capricorn/10th house

What is the forming, or evolving, emotional structure of the Soul? What specific dynamics represent the pull towards towards the future?

The North Node in Capricorn/10th house symbolizes that the evolving self-image of the Soul is based upon the need to establish a personal voice of authority in society, to accept responsibility for our actions, and mature emotionally. In so doing, the Soul will become determined to accomplish any life goal. The emotional shift from the past to the future will be felt in these areas.

The social role or career is a vehicle through which a personal voice of authority is expressed. We must all learn how society is structured and operates in order to gain the necessary certification(s) to assume a social position. This can lead to a natural maturation. Reflection upon the past will create the necessary awareness of dynamics that have become crystallized, outdated, and are preventing further growth. Emotional maturation takes hold through accepting responsibility for our own actions.

Maturity is also fostered through the actualization of a social role or career. Displaced emotions and dependencies of the past can be transmuted; the inner child becomes a healthy adult child. The experience of removing external sources of emotional security can enforce the same evolutionary lesson(s). In a natural expression, the Soul will encourage others to develop their own personal voice of authority in society, and mature emotionally through taking responsibility for their own actions.

Consensus State: In the Consensus State, the North Node in Capricorn/10th house will manifest as an evolving self-image that is based upon establishing a personal voice of authority within the mainstream society. The social role then becomes a means to mature emotionally and foster self-security outside the support or influence of the family environment (South Node in Cancer).

The Soul will desire to progress within the social strata. Most often, this will take hold through a specific social role or career within the mainstream. To do so, we must learn and conform to the prevailing social rules, laws, and customs within the culture or society of birth in order to advance. For example, to become a psychologist (in the US) one must complete seven years of school.

In a natural expression, the individual will emotionally mature through integration within the mainstream society, and holding a socially meaningful role in a responsible way. This reflects the pull towards the future. Conversely, the Soul could become dependent upon the authority of others or an external role in society to create emotional security, and use underhanded means to achieve personal ambitions and acquire social status.

Individuated State: In the Individuated State, the North Node in Capricorn/10th house will manifest as an evolving emotional structure that is based upon cultivating a personal voice of authority within an alternative field. The Soul will desire to individuate from the mainstream through actualizing a social role within an alternative field.

Emotional maturity takes hold as external dependencies upon others of like mind and those in the family environment are released (South Node in Cancer). As a reflection of the need to liberate from the mainstream, the Soul may align with an external social role that does not conform to the socially accepted gender assignments. For example, a man may decide to work in the field of child care which is typically considered a woman's role in the world. In so doing, self-authenticity and fostering a personal voice of authority that mirrors the intrinsic individuality manifests.

The key within this is to nurture an inner space of self-security (South Node in Cancer/4th house) in such a way that the natural voice of authority can be expressed independent from the mainstream society (North Node in Capricorn/10th house). The pull towards the future is felt in these ways. In turn, these Souls can motivate others by example to develop their own voice of authority, and to not be defined by the social roles within the mainstream. Conversely, the Soul may attempt to secure itself through conforming to the voices of others who hold a position of authority.

Spiritual State: In the Spiritual State, the North Node in Capricorn/10th house will manifest as a forming self-image that is rooted in the need to cultivate a personal voice of authority through union with the Creator, and an alignment with timeless, natural principles.

The forming self-image is rooted in the development of a personal voice of authority through a relationship with the God/dess. External emotional dependencies upon others within a spiritual community, group, or teacher are released as this emotional shift is made. Natural, universal laws become the foundation upon which the Soul nurtures its personal voice of authority, and materializes a meaningful social role.

The career, or social role will reflect the desire to serve the Source, and through reflection others. This potentially becomes a vehicle through which an integration of both the masculine and feminine, or the anima/animus takes hold. The individual may be perceived as a spiritual voice of authority, and via their example encourage others to develop their own voice of authority through the relationship with the Creator. The pull towards the future is felt in these ways.

**Famous people with
South Node in Cancer/4th house/
North Node in Capricorn/10th house:**

Ben Affleck

Gwyneth Paltrow

John Travolta

Pharrell Williams

South Node in Leo/5th house,
North Node in Aquarius/11th house

In order to discuss the core intentions of the South Node in Leo/5th house and the North Node in Aquarius/11th house we must first review the signs of Leo and Aquarius.

The sign of Leo corresponds to the need to creatively actualize and take control of the destiny through the strength of the will. As with all fire signs, Leo symbolizes a feeling of special destiny. Whereas in the archetype of Aries (the preceding fire sign) the special destiny was linked with a continual state of becoming and self discovery, in the sign of Leo the special destiny is known, complete, and is linked with creative actualization; to materialize all that we are.

It is through this sign that we become aware that we have something special to do in the world, a creative talent or capacity, and the desire to manifest our capacities to their fullest. As such, these individuals are most often natural creators, strong willed, and have an emotional need to take control of their destiny. In a distorted expression, delusions of self-grandeur can manifest relative to feeling of the special destiny and creative purpose.

Typically, a pyramid reality structure is created in which the individual's needs are at the very top, and all contributing life factors are expected to cater to these needs. This results in an overly self-centered focus on being the star or at the center of the world at all times.

All too often, giving only occurs relative to fulfillment of a personal need or agenda. The feeling of specialness results in an expectation for validation and recognition from others in the external environment. The need for this feedback can become constant. In some situations, whatever is given is never truly enough. The reason for this dynamic is the seed of insecurity that is symbolized in the preceding sign, Cancer.

The key here is to validate oneself from within instead of through the external environment. In this way, the dependency upon others to provide this feedback can be transmuted, and emotional self-empowerment developed. This dynamic is reflected in the natural square from Leo to the signs of Taurus (self-reliance) and Scorpio (transmutation).

Once the need for recognition and validation is internalized the true generosity of Leo can shine. In a natural expression, the Soul will validate the special capacities of others without feeling threatened and defensive, and encourage others to take charge of their destiny through the dynamic of self-empowerment.

The polarity sign of Leo is Aquarius. The sign of Aquarius symbolizes the need to liberate and decondition from the pyramid reality structure, and develop an objective awareness of life in general. Emotional detachment and disengagement leads to the necessary objectivity. In essence, by linking the special purpose to a socially relevant need, liberation from an overly subjective focus takes hold.

The individuated unconscious is reflected by this sign. Past life memories that are specific to the Soul are stored in the individuated unconsciousness, as well as memories that have been suppressed and repressed, as symbolized by the preceding sign of Capricorn. The individuated unconscious stores content that is unique to the individual, and information that pertains to the future.

The sign of Aquarius corresponds to trauma. Trauma can have many causes, and is intended to trigger the necessary detachment and objectivity previously described. In other words, we can use traumatic events to effect personal liberation and transformation. Post traumatic stress disorder, or unresolved trauma, is indicated. Projections are another dynamic symbolized by this sign. Projections manifest from the unconsciousness and can be linked with unresolved trauma.

The principle of like-mindedness corresponds to this sign. JWG teaches that there are three distinct social groups. One social group is the mainstream within any society or culture. Another social group is the alternative movement within society. A third social group are so-called social dinosaurs. Those in this social group advocate that a vision from the past be applied to modern times. A current example would be those who promote that we return to the racial, gender, and religious segregation of the past. Liberation takes hold through the release of emotional attachment from any social group, friendship, or relationship. The key within this is to stand as a group of one when necessary.

Now that we have reviewed the signs of both Leo and Aquarius, we can discuss the core intentions of the South Node in Leo/5th house and the North Node in Aquarius in the 11th house.

South Node in Leo/5th house

What is the self-image and emotional structure of the past symbolized by Leo in the 5th house? What specific dynamics constitute conscious emotional security relative to the past? The South Node in Leo/5th house reflects that the prior life personal lens is based upon creative actualization, subjective development, and self-empowerment.

Prior to the current life, the Soul most commonly created a pyramid reality structure in which its needs were at the very top, and a high degree of self-focus upon materialization of the special purpose and destiny. Typically, the individual has received some sort of special acknowledgment or recognition in the past, and this can result in the need for validation and acknowledgment from the external environment. In this situation, the Soul will need to be at the center of it all, or the start, at all times. No matter how much is given it is never really enough. This is because of an underlying insecurity symbolized in the preceding sign of Cancer. The intention is then to take control of the destiny and in so doing bring about emotional self-empowerment.

Coming into the current life, the individual will naturally orientate towards these same areas. The Soul will feel a sense of special destiny, and a desire to self-actualize. Creative talents and abilities are essential components of the prior life self-image. An overly subjective focus, the need for external validation and acknowledgment, the creation of a pyramid reality structure, are dynamics that represent the conscious emotional security of the past. As such, these are potential areas of limitation.

Consensus State: In the Consensus State, the South Node in Leo/5th house is expressed as a prior life emotional structure that is based upon materialization of a creative talent or capacity within the mainstream. The feeling of special destiny is linked to progression within the social strata.

Creative actualization of inbuilt capacities and talents then becomes a vehicle through which the Soul gets ahead of the system. For example, the individual may have a natural ability as a teacher, editor, or within any given field in the mainstream. In the best expression, this could become a potential avenue for manifestation of these intrinsic gifts and advancement within the mainstream to occur.

Typically, there is an over-identification with the creative abilities and purpose relative to the need for recognition from the external environment. In a natural expression, the Soul will use their special capacities to take charge of the destiny and progress within the social strata. However, some will actualize through delusions of personal grandeur and create a pyramid reality structure due to the emotional security that it brings.

Individuated State: In the Individuated State, the South Node in Leo/5th house is expressed as a prior life personal lens that is based upon materialization of the inbuilt and unique abilities within an alternative field. The feeling of special destiny is linked with actualization of unique special capacities outside the mainstream.

The manifestation of these capacities then becomes a means to individuate, and liberate from the mainstream society. Emotional self-empowerment will take hold as the individual self-actualizes in a way that reflects his or her individuality. In essence, the individual will break free from the mainstream through taking charge of the destiny within an alternative field. This, in turn, can motivate others do the same.

Spiritual State: In the Spiritual State, the South Node in Leo/5th house is expressed as a prior life emotional structure that is based upon self-actualization and self-empowerment through union with the Universal Source. The special destiny is linked with spiritual development, and alignment with natural, timeless principles reflected in the manifested Creation.

The Soul will emotionally self-empower through materialization of the inbuilt capacities that reflect the desire to serve the Source, and through extension, others.

The self-image is rooted in becoming a vehicle through which the creative principle flows, and a co-creator with the Source. In the best expression, the Soul will motivate others to self-empower via alignment with timeless, universal principles, merging with God/dess, and to use their special gifts to serve the Universal Source, and as a reflection others in some way. They may be seen in a special light by others relative the knowledge of natural laws.

The North Node in Aquarius/11th house

What is the evolving emotional structure of the Soul? What specific dynamics represent the shift towards the future? The North Node in Aquarius/11th house reflects a forming self-image that is based on the evolution from subjective to objective awareness, psychological detachment, and the need to individuate.

The intention is to become an observer of oneself and others, and integrate as a member of the community rather than "the star." The lesson is to stand alone if necessary in order for individuation and deconditioning to take hold. Emotional attachments are then released. Most often, there is a natural emotional need to connect with others of like mind.

The key within this is that the creative capacities and talents must be linked with a socially relevant need; the Soul will then progressively gain a more objective awareness of itself and life in general. This reflects the evolution from subjective reality to the objective awareness. Emotional detachment and disengagement also leads to objectivity and liberation from emotional attachment.

Consensus State: In the Consensus State, the North Node in Aquarius/11th house is expressed as an evolving emotional structure that is based upon the need to bond with like-minded others within the mainstream, liberate from the pyramid reality structure, and link the special destiny with a socially relevant need within the mainstream society.

For example, the individual could join a like-minded community within any given field within the consensus. The Soul's creative talents are then applied within this community (South Node in Leo/5th house, North Node in Aquarius/11th house). This serves as a vehicle through which the Soul gets ahead of the system. Liberation from delusions of self-grandeur, and the need for constant validation and acknowledgment from the external environment is affected through this emotional shift. The pull towards the future is felt in these areas.

Liberation from social groups within the mainstream that do not hold the same values as the Soul, and are not of like mind, must take place. In so doing, the individual will gain the ability to stand as a group of one if necessary. Conversely, the Soul may choose to actualize through delusions of self-grandeur due to the emotional security that is linked with this dynamic.

Individuated State: In the Individuated State, the North Node in Aquarius/11th house will manifest as a forming self-image that is based on the need to individuate from the mainstream society, and to bond with others of like mind in the alternative of society. The need is to link the creative abilities to a socially relevant need in an alternative field.

The key within this is to liberate from an over-identification with a special role and outdated emotional attachments within like-minded social group(s). In so doing, the individual will materialize their unique and special gifts within an alternative field (South Node in Leo/5th house, North Node in Aquarius/11th house). For example, in a positive expression, the Soul may join a like-minded alternative education community through which creative actualization takes place. In this way, special capabilities are used in a transformed way that reflects the Souls individuality. The pull towards the future is felt in these areas.

Spiritual State: In the Spiritual State, the North Node in Aquarius/11th house will manifest as an evolving emotional structure and personal lens that is based upon the need to individuate through union with the Source, and like-minded others who also seek to spiritualize.

In this evolutionary state, the individual will most often link his or her creativity with the needs of a spiritual community or group. The collective whole is served in this way (South Node in Leo/5th, North Node in Aquarius/11th house). The ideal of universal spiritual communities in which each individual spiritually develops through timeless, natural principles is symbolized.

The Soul will develop the ability to stand as a group of one, independent from any spiritual community or teacher as his or her special destiny is connected to serving a collective need. Prior to the current life, the individual may have held a special role within a spiritual group (South Node in Leo/5th house). Liberation from an over-identification with the role is symbolized by the North Node in Aquarius/11th house. The emotional shift towards the future is navigated in these ways.

**Famous people with
South Node in Leo/5th house/
North Node in Aquarius/11th house:**

Albert Einstein

Kristen Stewart

Jennifer Lawrence

Liam Neeson

South Node in Virgo/6th house,
North Node in Pisces/12th house

In order to discuss the core intentions of the South Node in Virgo/6th house and the North Node in Pisces/12th house we must first review the signs of Virgo and Pisces.

Virgo is a transitional sign. The transition from subjective development (Aries-Leo) to objective development (Libra-Pisces) is reflected here. In essence, the pyramid inverts itself, and we become aware of all we're lacking, or not. Self-adjustment, purification, and egocentric humility take hold as the balloon of self-inflation is pierced. Self-adjustment is felt in any dynamic that is linked with an overly subjective orientation symbolized by the proceeding signs of Aries-Leo. What is felt is "right" is linked with objective development and focus reflected in the following signs of Libra-Pisces

Virgo corresponds to service to the whole. We become aware of all our imperfections, impurities, faults, and desire to effect self-improvement relative to the need to serve the whole in some way. Crisis is often created in order induce the necessary inner adjustments. Positively responded to, crisis leads to self-awareness and knowledge. Negatively responded to, excessive crisis and an overly critical self-focus can create a state of perpetual self-undermining behavior.

In this situation, we make what appear to be logical excuses, rationalizations, as to why we are not "ready" or "perfect" enough to do the tasks we know we are capable of performing. The reason for this dynamic is that, all too often, there is an inner existential void that is more than an aloneness. Compensation for this void through a variety of avoidance and/or denial associated behavior then follows. For example, the busy bee syndrome can manifest in which the Soul is always engaged in external activities and obligations.

The need is to discern between the "apparent" and the "actual" reality. Crisis is often a means to trigger this essential lesson. For instance, a crisis may be experienced in regards to too many external obligations. The apparent reality for the crisis is not enough time to do what the Soul knows it needs to do for itself. The actual reality for the crisis is compensation for an inner aloneness/emptiness. Positively responded to, self-knowledge is gained as the individual becomes aware of the actual reasons for the creation of the crisis.

The psychology of sado-masochism is symbolized here. The seeds of sado-masochism are contained within the Garden of Eden myth. In this myth women are presented as the spiritual downfall, or temptation, of men. Women are made to feel guilty and inferior, and feel the need to atone for the guilt. This reflects the pathology of the masochism. Men are made to feel guilty, superior, and the resulting need to punish, or get back at others comes as a reaction to the guilt. This reflects the pathology of sadism. Typically, women embody masochism while men embody sadism.

However, these two psychologies can exist simultaneously, and fluctuate, within the same person. Victimization corresponds to this sign.

The polarity sign of Virgo is Pisces. The sign of Pisces corresponds to the need to align with a transcendent reality, for ultimate meaning, and merge with the Source of All Things. It is the combination, or composite, of all the preceding signs put together. It signifies where we are susceptible to delusions and illusions, and also where we can become inspired by God/dess.

This sign indicates that a culmination of an entire evolutionary cycle is underway. In a natural expression, an overly critical self-focus, excessive crisis, victimization, and sado-masochistic psychology can be brought to closure. "Right work", and a relationship with the Source replaces the existential void relative to the need for ultimate meaning. When ultimate meaning is projected externally, in whatever area of life, we experience disillusionment. Disillusionment is one of the most painful of all emotions, yet it serves to align us with actual reality (Virgo).

The potential for escapism is signified here. A loss of meaning can trigger the need to escape. One form of escape is substance abuse. Another is through the creation of fantasies and illusions. For instance, the individual may attempt to escape through imagining or pretending to be character within a movie, book, or of their own creation. In this way, fantasy becomes reality. Deception can then occur. Of course, we may be deceived by others. This dynamic occurs when we focus on the "potential" of others, yet do not see their actual reality clearly. We then become disillusioned. As mentioned previously, disillusionment is intended to align us with actual reality.

As the individual acts to spiritualize and embraces timeless, universal principles as reflected in the totality of Creation the need to escape from reality will be purged from the Soul. Illusions and delusions will be eliminated, and the painful experiences of disillusionment will subside. A higher cause or purpose can be a means to establish ultimate meaning within the overall life.

Charities, humanitarian causes, and non-profit organizations are all examples of higher causes. The key within this is that ultimate meaning must be defined from within instead of externally in whatever area of life. The underlying need is to merge the emotional body with the Eternal to internalize ultimate meaning. The sign of Pisces corresponds with the transfer from deductive logic to inductive logic. Deductive logic attempts to build the whole out of all the individual parts. Inductive logic focuses upon the whole first, and then allows all the individual parts to naturally fit into place. In this way, simplification within the overall life takes hold.

Now that we have reviewed the signs of Virgo and Pisces, we can discuss the core intentions of the South Node in Virgo/6th house, and the North Node in Pisces/12th house. What is the prior life emotional structure of the Soul symbolized by the South Node in Virgo in the 6th house? What are the specific dynamics that represent conscious emotional security relative to the past?

The South Node in Virgo/6th house

The South Node in Virgo/6th house reflects that the prior life self-image is based upon the need to be of service to the whole, to self-perfect, and to foster personal humility. Most commonly on coming into the life the individual will be highly self-critical and prone to crisis and self-analysis. The psychology of victimization is also reflected in this South Node placement. These are the dynamics from the past that constitute emotional security and can create limitations.

Prior to the current life, the Soul has experienced an inverted pyramid in which its needs are at the very bottom. This serves to pierce the balloon of self-inflation, and cultivate personal humility. Essentially, the individual has become aware of all their imperfections, lacks and faults. This can create self-undermining behavior which manifests as perpetual excuses as to why they are not good enough or ready enough to do the "right work," or what they know they are capable of doing. The psychology of masochism, or sadism, or both, is symbolized as well.

Typically, the individual will be quite self-effacing, humble, and helpful. Service to the underdogs, or those who have been marginalized or persecuted, is a natural point of gravitation for many of these Souls, however, the individual may become excessively critical in some situations, and project an overall negative attitude in the environment. This is based upon an inwardly negative and self-critical focus.

The "busy bee" syndrome can manifest in which the individual is engaged in constant external activity and excessive obligations in order to fill the inner existential void. Crisis then results, which can lead to the necessary self-awareness and adjustments. These individuals have an innate capacity to help others who are in a state of crisis, and most often respond to those who have felt victimized by life in general.

Consensus State: In the Consensus State, the South Node in Virgo/6th house will manifest as a prior life emotional structure that is based upon the need to serve to the whole, to self-perfect and improve within the mainstream society. Most often, the Soul will desire to advance within society through improvement and perfection of existing techniques and the work function within the mainstream.

These individuals will be highly critical towards those that do not conform to the mainstream society, and reject any techniques that are outside the socially accepted practices. In a natural expression, the Soul may desire to help others within the mainstream society who have been under served or privileged in some way via improving the overall life conditions. However, in a distorted expression, some may undermine this capacity and perform mundane work just to get by, and to keep busy.

Individuated State: In the Individuated State, this will manifest as a prior life emotional structure that is founded upon the need to serve the whole and effect self-improvement within an alternative field. Most often, the

Soul will desire to individuate from the mainstream through a unique form of service that reflects the Soul's individuality.

Self-improvement and perfection are relative to the release of self-undermining and compensatory emotional patterns that are linked with conformity to the mainstream. In other words, the individual may deny the need to liberate due to a fear of rejection. Most commonly, prior to the current life these individuals have experienced persecution from others for not conforming to the consensus. This may be re-experienced coming in the current life (South Node in Virgo/6th house). Of course, the Soul may be overly critical of those who conform. The key within this is to suggest techniques for improvement as necessary, instead of issuing critical statements.

In a natural expression, the Soul will desire to be of service to those of like mind and also seek to individuate. In this situation, the individual may align with a life path that is centered upon service to those who have been persecuted and/or rejected for being different, and allows liberation to take hold. Conversely, the individual may reject the need to individuate and undermine their unique form of service by either performing mundane work, or always keeping busy enough to avoid an inner emptiness or fear of persecution.

Spiritual State: In the Spiritual State, the South Node in Virgo/6th house will manifest as a prior emotional structure and self-image that is based upon service to the whole and self-improvement through union with the Universal Source. The Soul will desire to serve others as a reflection of service to God/dess.

In this evolutionary condition, "right work" is centered upon alignment with natural, timeless, principles as reflected in the manifested Creation. Commonly, the Soul will not feel ready or perfect enough to do the tasks as directed by the Source which then leads to perpetual excuse-making, and self-undermining behavior. The antidote to this situation is to readjust the notion of "perfection" as a process that occurs one step at a time.

The key knowledge contained within this is that the Source is not inherently perfect, rather in an evolving state of perfection, simultaneously perfect/imperfect. In other words, in a natural expression, these individuals will motivate others to align with their right work, and to effect self-improvement through union with the Universal Source. The motto becomes "just try to be a little bit better every day, and if you don't make it, just wake up the next day and try again."

North Node in Pisces/12th house

What is the forming emotional structure of the Soul? What are the specific dynamics that represent the pull towards the future? The North Node in Pisces/12th house symbolizes that the evolving emotional structure and self-image is based upon the need to establish ultimate meaning from within, embrace a transcendent reality, and dissolve old emotional patterns that are linked with a negative and critical self-focus.

Emotional union with God/dess is a vehicle through which the Soul completes an entire evolutionary cycle, and cultivates ultimate meaning from within. Sado-masochistic psychology and victimization is then dissolved, so growth continues. Disillusionment and a loss of personal meaning may occur to trigger these intentions. These are the central dynamics that represent the emotional shift to the future, and the foundation of the developing self-image.

Transcendent values and principles will progressively replace temporal values as the Soul merges the emotional body with the eternal. Illusions and delusions are released, and right work replaces mundane work, as are numerous external activities that serve just to keep the individual busy. Excessive crisis is then eliminated, and the existential void is filled through cultivating a relationship with the Creator.

A higher cause or purpose is a means to foster ultimate meaning and materialize right work. Self-forgiveness and compassion replaces a negative and critical focus. A simplification within the overall life will take hold. The Soul will develop inductive logic which first grasps the whole and allows all the individual parts to naturally fall into place.

As the Soul emotionally re-unites with the natural God/dess, the realization that the Source is not inherently perfect, but simultaneously perfect/imperfect, evolving perfection is felt.

As JWG taught, how can a perfect anything create an imperfect anything? The lyrics of the late Leonard Cohen, who has South Node in Virgo and North Node in Pisces, serve to illustrate the emotional shift from the evolutionary past to the future reflected by this nodal axis, "There is a crack in everything, that's how the light comes in."

Consensus State: In the Consensus State, the North Node in Pisces/12th house will manifest as an evolving emotional structure and self-image that is based upon an alignment with transcendent principles and reality within the mainstream society. A culmination of avoidance-orientated activity such as the busy bee syndrome, and mundane work just to get away will take hold. In other words, self-undermining emotional patterns of the past linked with the need to manifest right work must dissolve. In so doing, alignment with a higher purpose for the life takes hold (South Node in Virgo/6th house/North Node in Pisces/12th house).

For example, non-profit organizations, charities, and humanitarian causes are all potential expressions of right work and reflect an alignment with ultimate meaning within the mainstream. In this way, The Soul will simplify its overall life through elimination of excessive external activities and obligations. In this evolutionary state, the individual will advance within the system through actualization of right work within the mainstream society that is an alignment with a higher cause/purpose. The pull towards the future is felt in these areas.

Individuated State: In the Individuated State, the North Node in Pisces/12th house will manifest as an evolving emotional structure that is based upon the need to embrace a transcendent reality and principles within an alternative field. The underlying emotional need is to liberate from mainstream society through alignment with universal, timeless laws that go beyond the socially accepted mainstream notions of what reality is and is not, and reflect the inherent individuality within the Soul.

Culmination of past emotional patterns linked with denial and rejection of the individuation impulse must occur in order for evolution to proceed. In so doing, right work can become a vehicle through which the Soul nurtures the need to merge with the Universal Source and individuate.

For example, various forms of alternative healing such as regression therapy, meditation, dream journals, and yoga are possible expressions of right work that are in alignment with a higher purpose within an alternative field (South Node in Virgo/6th house/North Node in Pisces/12th house). In this way, past experiences of persecution and rejection are brought to a close. In turn, the Soul can motivate others to heal from these same experiences through their example. The emotional shift towards the future is reflected in these areas.

Spiritual State: In the Spiritual State, the North Node in Pisces/12th house is expressed as an evolving emotional structure and self-image that is founded upon the need to merge with the Source and align with natural, timeless principles. Spiritual development takes hold through the culmination of past dynamics linked with self-undermining behavior which negates, or blocks, that actualization of right work as directed by the Source.

For example, constant excuses as to why the individual is not ready or perfect enough to do the work as directed by God/dess must be released. The existential void can then be filled through fostering a relationship with the Source. Right work will reflect the desire to serve Source in some way, using the Soul's knowledge of natural, universal principles.

Ultimate meaning is nurtured from within via a primary relationship with the Source, and alignment with universal, timeless laws. In the words of the great Swami Sri Yukteswar, "Every saint has a past, and every sinner has a future." The pull towards the future is felt in these ways.

**Famous people with
South Node in Virgo/6th house,
North Node in Pisces/12th house:**

Gwen Stefani

Robin Williams

Adele

Matt Damon

South Node in Libra/7th house,
North Node in Aries/1st house

In order to discuss the core intentions of the South Node in Libra/7th house, and the North Node in Aries/1st house we must revisit the signs of both Aries and Libra.

The sign of Libra corresponds with the initiation of relationships with others, and emergence into the social realm. It signifies expectations, and the need to give to others, the need to be given to, and projected needs within relationships. The natural law of giving, sharing, and inclusion is indicated.

Libra reflects that a state of extremity has been reached, and the resulting need to learn balance relative to such extremity must be addressed. The principles of equality, justice, and fair play are symbolized. It is through comparison and contrast with others that we evaluate our own identity, who we are, who we are not, and cannot be. We are exposed to the dynamic of relativity through the initiation of relationships with others. We learn about the diversity of needs, values, beliefs, and realities of others, and which realities reflect our own, and which do not.

It is when we lose touch with our needs and identity that we create imbalances and extremities within relationships. As an example of such extremities, one partner may play a subservient role to the other. In this situation, the individual will fulfill the needs of the partner to the exclusion of their own. In this way, the individual becomes a vicarious extension of the reality, needs, identity of the partner. The other extreme is the dominant role. In this situation, the individual will reinforce his or her or own needs and expectations in such a way that the other feels by meeting them their own needs are being fulfilled.

These roles can be static or fluctuate within the same relationship. Both partners are co-dependent upon each other relative to these roles. The core dynamic that creates such imbalances is the need to be needed. A variation of this theme is student/teacher and/or counselor/client.

The sign of Libra corresponds with the psychology of listening. The need to achieve balance and equality requires that we learn to listen to others objectively, as they speak from their reality. In this way, we can identify reality as it exists for others in general. In other words, the initiation of relationships with others sets up the need to listen objectively instead of from our own subjective filter, or from our own reality. In so doing, we then know what to give and what not to give, and who reflects our overall reality and who does not.

A key lesson within this is when to give and when not to. In essence, it is to learn that by in certain situations withholding, or appearing not to give, we are practicing a supreme form of giving. These situations will always involve withholding giving when the other has not applied what has already been given, yet asks for more. In this way, co-dependencies and imbalances can be purged, and a balanced state of equal giving and receiving can take place.

The polarity sign of Libra is Aries. The sign of Aries corresponds to a brand new evolutionary cycle, and the need for freedom and independence in order to discover what this new cycle is about. This sign reflects a continuous state of becoming which is universally experienced.

It is though the initiation of action that self-discovery takes place. Learning occurs on an action/reaction basis. The analogy that is given to us by JWG to illustrate this point is a baby that touches a hot stove: the baby takes action, touching the stove, and in the reaction to that touch, it's hot, the implied knowledge is gained. This need requires an essential freedom and independence in order to generate whatever experience is deemed necessary in order for self-discovery to take place. In essence, we learn to ask and answer our own questions from within, and to initiate one's own life path or direction without asking consent or permission from another. Most often there is an instinctive anger towards any restriction of personal freedom.

The sign of Aries symbolizes our instincts. The new evolutionary cycle is put into motion through instinctual response to an immediate experience. In other words, we may be instinctively attracted to a new experience, person, opportunity, etc. Conversely, we may be instinctively repelled by any given life event. The key point within is that by honoring our instincts in both situations self-discovery occurs.

This sign corresponds to fear. Fear have many causes, and may lead to a resistance towards initiating, or acting upon, the necessary experiences that would lead to a new evolutionary cycle. If we make choices that are based on fear, acting only upon what is known and familiar, the past is then recycled into the future. Positively, if we act to break free from fear a new evolutionary cycle is put into motion - for example, a new cycle within relationships that is based upon mutual independence and equality.

Now that we have reviewed the signs of Libra and Aries, we can discuss the core evolutionary intentions of the South Node in Libra/7th house, and the North Node in Aries/1st house.

The South Node in Libra/7th house

What is the prior emotional structure of the past? What are the specific dynamics that represent the conscious emotional security of the past? The South Node in Libra/7th house symbolizes that the prior life self-image is based upon the initiation of relationships, the need to be needed, the need to learn balance and equality, and the principles of justice and fair play. These are the core dynamics that constitute the conscious emotional security patterns of the past.

Coming into the life, the Soul will naturally gravitate towards these dynamics. and will desire to initiate a diversity of relationships in order to learn through comparison and contrast about their own identity. The need to listen to others objectively, to understand what to give and what not to give is signified. All too often, the individual will desire to accommodate the reality of the partner in such a way that he or she loses sight of their own identity and needs. In the best expression, these Souls can be natural counselors with an innate capacity to listen. The axiom "do unto others as you would have done onto yourself" is a guiding principle within the overall life.

Typically, co-dependencies, imbalances and extremes are patterns of past behavior that are creating blocks towards further evolution. The reason for this dynamic is the need to be needed. A key lesson within this is to learn when to give, and when not to give. In so doing, a supreme form of giving is practiced through appearing not to give in certain situations.

Consensus State: In the Consensus State, the South Node in Libra/7th house will manifest as a prior life emotional structure that is based upon initiation of relationships with others within the mainstream society.

The Soul will form relationships with others within the mainstream society in order to gain the necessary knowledge as to how to advance within the system. For example, the individual may initiate relationships with those at a higher social position within a given field to learn how to progress. The Soul will expect that others conform to the socially accepted norms of behavior, and conventional roles within relationships. The individual will listen and evaluate others relative to these social norms and expectations.

In a natural expression, the Soul will use the social system and relationships to give back to others in some way. For instance, the individual could help others through advocating equal rights and a social system that supports justice, fair play and equality. In this case, the Soul can potentially mentor others who also seek to progress within the social strata(s). Conversely, the individual will promote that existing inequalities and inequalities be sustained relative to the wealth, etc. In other words, in a negative expression that individual will seek to maintain an unjust and unequal social system. This is due to the emotional security that is derived from these emotional patterns.

Individuated State: In the Individuated State, the South Node in Libra/7th house will manifest as a prior emotional structure that is based upon initiation of relationships with others of like mind who also desire to individuate from the mainstream. The Soul will form relationships with others in order to facilitate liberation and deconditioning from the socially accepted norms, expectations, and traditional roles within relationships. Typically, a dependency upon others relative to the need to break free from the status quo has been created prior to the current life.

In this evolutionary condition the Soul will rebel against traditional relationships and expectations within the mainstream, and seek to establish role equality and interchangeability. As such, the individual will need to learn to listen and evaluate others relative to the need to individuate, and free themselves from relationships that reinforce mainstream expectations and socially accepted behavior. In so doing, the Soul will then know who to form relationships with and who not. Conversely, the Soul may sustain co-dependencies in which the need to individuate is projected externally due to the emotional security that is linked with these past emotional patterns.

Spiritual State: In the Spiritual State, the South Node in Libra/7th house is expressed as an emotional structure that is based upon initiation of relationships with others who also desire to merge with the Source. The Soul will form relationships with others in order to facilitate the need to spiritualize.

The underlying need is to cultivate a primary relationship with God/dess, and timeless, natural principles. These central dynamics are the foundation upon which the Soul spiritually develops, and evaluates which relationships to initiate and which not. In a positive expression, the natural law of giving, sharing, and inclusion will become the bottom line within relationships.

Most commonly, the individual has become dependent upon others in the context of spiritual knowledge. In other words, the Soul may have attracted spiritual "teacher types" prior to the current life. The Soul will seek to counteract, or balance, such extremes by initiating relationships in which the need to spiritualize is equal and a dynamic of mutual teacher/ student is shared by both partners.

North Node in Aries/1st house

What is the evolving self-image of the Soul? What are the specific dynamics that represent the pull towards the future? The North Node in Aries/1st house reflects that the forming personal lens is founded upon the development of the independent voice, the ability to seek one's own questions from within, and for the opportunity to self-discovery/recovery to be created.

An emotional paradox is reflected by this nodal axis because these individual needs must be balanced with the need for relationship. These dynamics symbolize the gravitational shift from the past towards the future.

Freedom and independence is required in order to generate whatever experiences are deemed necessary for self-discovery to take place. A sense of special destiny is felt in the context of a new evolutionary cycle. As the Soul begins to develop its own independent voice, mutual independence and equality within relationships will take hold (South Node in Libra/7th house, North Node in Aries/1st house). The previously described emotional paradox linked with relationships is resolved in this way.

Dependencies of the past will be transmuted through the initiation of independent action and without waiting for the other to take action first. In other words, relationships founded upon the mutual independent actualization of both partners will be created as the Soul strikes out on its own, and develops the capacity to ask and answer its own questions from within. The bottom line within relationships then becomes "I am here because I want to be, not because I need to be." In so doing, a new evolutionary cycle is put into motion.

Consensus State: In the Consensus State, the North Node in Aries/1st house will manifest as an evolving self-image that is based upon the development of the independent voice within the mainstream. The Soul will need freedom and independence in order to initiate whatever experiences are deemed necessary to advance within society. The individual will gain the ability to ask and answer their own questions within the context of mainstream society (South Node in Libra/7th, North Node in Aries/1st house).

For example, the Soul could strike out on its own within the mainstream society in such a way that it breaks new ground within a given field. The individual will have the ability to pioneer a new direction within the consensus. Self-discovery is linked with progression through the social strata. In a positive expression, a new evolutionary cycle is put into motion as the Soul establishes relationships that are founded upon mutual independence, and discovers its own voice within the mainstream. The emotional shift to the future will be felt in these areas.

Conversely, some may act based on fear and recycle the past into the future in such a way that a new cycle does not manifest. For example, the Soul can sustain the dependencies of the past and bring these emotional patterns into the future. This is due to the emotional security that is derived from these dynamics.

Individuated State: In the Individuated State, the North Node in Aries/1st house will manifest as an evolving emotional structure that is based on the development of the independent voice within an alternative field; it needs freedom and independence in order to act upon the individuation impulse.

Self-discovery is linked with liberation from the mainstream. In a positive expression, the Soul will independently actualize the unique individuality. In this way, relationships founded upon mutual independence and equality will take hold. In essence, liberation from co-dependencies and imbalances within relationships occurs through independent action upon the need to individuate (South Node in Libra/7th house, North Node in Aries/1st house).

For instance, the individual could pioneer a new direction, or break new ground within an alternative field. In so doing, a new evolutionary cycle is put into motion. In a natural expression, these Souls will encourage others to do what they must in order to discover or recover themselves, independent from mainstream society. This reflects the pull towards the future. Conversely, the individual may recycle the relationship patterns of the past into the future by maintaining co-dependency and not acting independently.

Spiritual State: In the Spiritual State, the North Node in Aries/1st house is expressed as an evolving emotional structure that is based upon the development of the independent voice through merging with the Source.

The Soul will need freedom and independence in order to initiate whatever actions are deemed necessary for spiritual growth to occur. Self-discovery is linked with alignment with timeless, universal principles. In essence, it is to learn to act independently upon the need to spiritualize outside the influence of any relationship, spiritual community, group, or teacher.

In so doing, dependencies upon spiritual teacher types are purged. Relationships founded upon the mutually independent spiritual development of both partners then follow. This is reflected by the South Node in Libra/7th house, and the North Node in Aries/1st house.

A new evolutionary cycle begins as the Soul discovers/recovers itself through union with God/dess, and becomes aware of natural laws. These individuals will encourage others to act upon the desire to know and merge with the Source, and to align with natural laws through direct experience. The emotional shift to the future then takes hold.

**Famous people with
South Node in Libra/7th house,
North Node in Aries/1st house:**

Sigmund Freud

Carl Jung

Meryl Streep

Rosa Parks

South Node in Scorpio/8th house, North Node in Taurus/2nd house

In order to discuss the core evolutionary intentions of the South Node in Taurus/2nd house and the North Node in Scorpio/8th house we must first revisit the signs of Scorpio and Taurus.

The sign of Scorpio corresponds to the natural principle of evolution. It symbolizes the need to transmute current limitations in order for growth to occur. This sign signifies the dynamics of cooperation and resistance. We can cooperate with the necessary changes or we can resist due to the emotional security that is linked with sustaining past patterns of behavior. Resistance creates stagnation and degeneration. Conversely, cooperation creates positive change, evolution, and regeneration.

The sign of Scorpio signifies psychological knowledge and development. In other words, the "why" of things must be understood. It is through the understanding of the why that we can identify the causes of our current limitations and grow beyond them.

The occult and that which is considered taboo are reflected by this sign. Attraction to the taboo can potentially become a vehicle through which transformation occurs. We become aware of universal forces and desire to unite with these forces. Evolution occurs as we merge with a higher source of power. It is important to note that power can be used positively to empower oneself and others, or negatively for manipulative purposes. As such, the proper use of power is a critical lesson here.

Experiences of power and powerlessness correspond to the sign of Scorpio. All too often, the rug of emotional security is pulled out from under our feet in order to effect evolution. This occurs through the removal of dynamics that have become limited and are causing stagnation; fears of abandonment, betrayal, and loss commonly result. Misapplication of trust is a core cause of this experience. The need is to learn who to trust, and who not to. Commitment within relationships can then take place.

In this way, fears of the past can be purged, and true intimacy will occur. In a natural expression, the Soul will encourage others to transmute their limitations in a non-manipulative manner. In a distorted expression, the Soul will attempt to manipulate others through the psychological knowledge of their weakest links.

The polarity sign of Scorpio is Taurus: the sign of Taurus correlates with the need to become self-reliant, self-sufficient, and to withdraw into the self in order to identify the inner resources necessary to effect survival. In essence, we must withdraw from the impact of the environment to root our identity and consolidate. In this way, we internalize the need for growth, and look within for the source of power to create transmutation (Scorpio).

The sign of Taurus reflects the inner nature of Venus, and our inner relationship with ourselves; the intention is to become self-reliant and self-sustaining and what we value for survival purposes will be given a high degree of meaning. This sign corresponds with the survival instinct, and within this is the instinct to procreate to ensure the survival of the species. As such, the Soul's sexual values and inner orientation towards sexuality are signified by the sign of Taurus.

Self-effort is a key here. In a distorted expression, this can manifest as laziness and inertia. In this situation, the individual will either vicariously live through others, or allow others to live vicariously through him or herself. In a natural expression, the individual will encourage others to make the effort to actualize their inner resources in order to effect self-reliance.

The sign of Taurus typically corresponds to the "frog in well" dynamic. From the bottom of the well, the frog has identified a small piece of the sky, yet thinks this is the whole universe. In this situation, the individual limits him or herself to an inner resource(s) that has been identified for survival (the frog in the well). Through internal or external confrontation (Scorpio) a necessary deepening takes hold through merging their resources with others in a compatible way. In so doing, the frog is forced from the well, and exposed to more of the sky.

Now that we have reviewed the signs of Scorpio and Taurus we can discuss the core evolutionary intentions of the South Node in Scorpio and the North Node in Taurus. What is the prior life emotional structure of the Soul? What specific dynamics represent the conscious emotional security of the past?

The South Node in Scorpio/8th house

The South Node in Scorpio/8th house symbolizes the prior life self-lens need to transmute limitations of past that are inhibiting further evolution, to develop a psychological understanding of oneself and life in general, and to merge with a higher source of power. The sign of Scorpio evokes deeper levels of awareness. In this way, the frog will jump from the well, and be exposed to more of sky.

In a natural expression, prior to the current life the Soul has learned to merge its resources and overall life in such a way that both individuals grow and evolve beyond what they were. In a distorted expression, the individual will form unions with others in order to gain power for egocentric/manipulative means. This sign signifies the dynamic of commitment, and making a choice as to who to commit to and who not. A deepening of the Soul occurs as the "whys," or core reasons of any given life circumstance are understood. In this way, patterns of the past that are inhibiting further growth are transmuted.

Coming into the life, the underlying intention is to identify the cause, or root, of the current limitations, and metamorphose beyond them. In this way, necessary psychological knowledge is gained. This knowledge can be used to effect continued evolution, and encourage others to do the same. Merging with a higher power propels evolution, and creates an awareness of deeper levels. Of course, this is relative to evolutionary state.

Consensus State: In the Consensus State, the South Node in Scorpio/8th house is expressed as a prior emotional structure that is based upon the need to transmute limitations of past that are inhibiting further evolution within the mainstream, develop a psychological understanding of how society is structured and operates, and to merge with others in such a way that advancement within society takes place.

Power will be linked with the social position and status. For example, the Soul could acquire psychological knowledge from relationships with those who hold positions of high status. In a natural expression, the individual will use this knowledge to evolve beyond its current limitations, and to help others progress through the social strata(s).

The Soul will desire to self-empower through psychological knowledge within the mainstream, and to merge with others in such a way that both people evolve. In a distorted expression, the knowledge of how society operates is used for manipulative purposes. For instance, the individual could abuse his or her social power for self-gain. This is due to the emotional security that is linked with these past emotional patterns.

Individuated State: In the Individuated State, the South Node in Scorpio/8th house is expressed as a prior emotional structure that is rooted in the need to transmute limitations of the past relative to liberation from the psychology of the mainstream, merge with those who are also seeking to individuate, and emotionally/psychologically "deepen" through individuation.

The Soul will desire to foster emotional transmutation through alternative psychological knowledge. For example, Jungian psychology and past life regression can be used to individuate and evolve out of past patterns that are inhibiting further evolution. The Soul will seek answers that go deeper than mainstream explanations, and resist conventional psychology. Attraction to the occult can reflect the desire to individuate, and to grow past old limitations.

In a natural expression, the individual will motivate others through their example to self-empower via alternative psychology that reflects the unique individuality. Fears of abandonment, betrayal and loss will be overcome, and commitment to others who also desire to liberate occurs. In so doing, the Soul will merge with others within alternative fields in such a way that metamorphosis takes hold. This reflects the emotional shift towards the future. In a negative expression, the Soul will resist the need to individuate and will sustain the limitations of the past.

Spiritual State: In the Spiritual State, the South Node in Scorpio/8th house will manifest as a prior emotional structure that is based on the need to transmute limitations through union with the Source, and develop psychological knowledge of universal, timeless, principles.

Most often, the individual will understand spiritual archetypes as they relate to the evolution of the Soul. Commitment to consistent spiritualization is a key dynamic as is alignment with natural, universal laws, which can enable metamorphosis beyond limitations. These principles are the foundation of the Soul's psychology.

Union with the Universal Source is the primary means to purge past patterns of behavior that are creating blocks towards evolution. In this way, a deepening of the Soul occurs. In a natural expression, the individual will motivate others to self-empower through spiritual development. The Soul will merge with others who also desire to unite with God/dess in such a way that an evolution for both partners takes hold. The emotional shift to the future is felt in these areas.

North Node in Taurus/2nd house

What is the forming emotional structure of the Soul? What dynamics represent the shift towards the evolutionary future? The North Node in Taurus/2nd house symbolizes that the evolving self-image is based upon the need to become self-reliant, to consolidate, and to identify inner resources to effect survival. The individual is purging outdated aspects of themselves in order to ground into their essence, or root.

Typically, the Soul will be thrown back on itself in some way in order to enforce the necessary lessons for this self-reliance and sufficiency. (South Node in Scorpio/8th house) The individual will withdraw inwardly in order to ground into their essence free from any external influence.

The sign of Taurus reflects our relationship with our self, our values and resulting sense of meaning in life. Simplification occurs as the Soul purges and eliminates outdated aspects that are preventing further growth. Any dynamic that the individual no longer finds relevant, or cannot relate to, will be purged. In this way, an alignment with the Soul's inner values takes hold (North Node in Taurus/2nd house). The key within this effort is to actualize their inner resources in order to become self-sustaining. How this process takes place is dependent on the evolutionary state/condition.

Consensus State: In the Consensus State, the North Node in Taurus will manifest as an evolving emotional structure that is based upon the need to identify inner resources to effect survival, and to cultivate self-sufficiency within the mainstream society. The Soul will desire to get ahead of the system and gain the psychological knowledge of how society is structured and operates in order to advance (South Node in Scorpio/8th house, North Node in Taurus/2nd house).

For example, the individual may utilize his or her own skills within an existing field in such a way as to become self-sustaining, and as a result will only relate to others who hold their same values. Those who do not will be excluded. In a natural expression, the Soul will encourage the development of reliance on oneself and others, and promote the values of personal effort and self-worth. This reflects the shift towards the future. In a distorted expression, the Soul will use the resources to achieve social status, wealth, etc (South Node in Scorpio, North Node in Taurus/2nd house).

Individuated State: In the Individuated State, the North Node in Taurus/2nd house is expressed as a evolving emotional structure that is based upon the need to identify inner resources in order to affect survival and self-sufficiency within an alternative field.

The Soul will desire to liberate from the values of mainstream, and form bonds with like-minded others who also seek to individuate. Progressive feelings of isolation from the values of the mainstream serve to ignite the underlying emotional need to individuate. For some, this is can manifest as becoming a minimalist. In this situation, the individual adopts the attitude that "less is more."

In a positive expression, the individual will manifest the inner resources that reflect his or her individuality. These resources can be used to create survival and self-reliance within an alternative field. The Soul will highly value individuality, and not relate to the overall lifestyle and orientation promoted within the mainstream society. As such, the individual must make the effort to individuate from within themselves, independent from the resources or influence of others.

In a positive expression, the Soul will then encourage through their own example others to manifest inner resources that are symbolic of their individuality, and to become self-sustaining within an alternative field. In so doing, the emotional shift to the future takes hold. In a negative expression, the Soul will resist the need to individuate by not making the necessary effort do to so, and may live vicariously through the values/resources of others.

The Spiritual State: In the Spiritual State, The North Node in Taurus/2nd house is expressed as an evolving emotional structure that is based upon the need to become self-sufficient through union with the Source. A primary relationship with God/dess will become a vehicle through which self reliance and independence will take hold. Timeless, universal principles are the foundation of the value system and the Soul's inner relationship with itself.

The key within this is the self-effort required to spiritualize in such as way that the need to merge with a higher source of power is internalized rather than sought through powerful spiritual teacher types or others (South Node in Scorpio, North Node in Taurus). In so doing, self-sufficiency is energized.

In a positive expression, the individual will then encourage others to cultivate a primary relationship with God/dess as a means to cultivate self-reliance, and to materialize inner resources that are in alignment with universal, natural Laws. This reflects the pull towards the future.

**Famous people with
South Node in Scorpio/8th house/
North Node in Taurus/2nd house:**

Hillary Clinton
Martin Luther King
Kurt Cobain
Billy Corgan
Paramahansa Yogananda

South Node in Sagittarius/9th house,
North Node in Gemini/3rd house

In order to discuss the core evolutionary intentions of the South Node in Sagittarius/9th house and North Node in Gemini/3rd house we must review the signs of Sagittarius and Gemini.

The sign of Sagittarius corresponds with the need to understand life in a metaphysical, cosmological/philosophical context, which in turn gives rise to belief systems. Belief is the determinant of how we interpret any given life situation.

There is a vast difference between a "belief" and actual knowledge, or natural law, which is based on direct experience. For example, I do not need a belief to know that the sky is blue, I simply know it to be true. It is through this sign that we become aware of natural laws and principles as reflected in the manifested Creation. Natural laws explain how the manifested Creation operates, and as such are self-evident.

The sign of Sagittarius symbolizes the intuitive component within consciousness which is governed by the right brain. The intuition knows what it knows without necessarily knowing how it knows. The intellect does not know what is true and not true; this is a function of the intuition. Truth is not a product of the intellect or belief; it inherently exists in and of itself.

The need to align with both personal truth and natural law and eliminate delusive beliefs is indicated. The resulting need is for freedom and the independence to discover one's personal truth, and any restriction of freedom for this to take place will not be tolerated. As with all fire signs, there is a sense of special destiny. The special destiny is linked with the discovery of personal truth.

The principle of perpetual expansion and growth is indicated here. Expansion occurs as the Soul progressively embraces more and more of the total truth. In this way, the individual will eliminate delusive beliefs via alignment with timeless, natural principles that are universally experienced, and will be true regardless of the passage of time. This is symbolized by the square of Sagittarius to the sign of Pisces.

In a natural expression, the Soul will encourage others to discover their personal truth and promote intuitive development. In a distorted expression, the individual will attempt to convince and convert others due to the emotional security that is linked with their beliefs. This has been described as the "Billy Graham" or preacher archetype.

One of the deepest correspondences is to the Daemon archetype. This describes when consciousness in human form has fused, or merged with plants and animals in such a way that it becomes a messenger of God/dess. In the context of the dynamics of belief and interpretation, this archetype has been represented by the Christian religion as the Demon. The symbol of Sagittarius is the centaur, which is half-man and half-horse. The original interpretation of this symbol as reflected by natural law is fusion with nature, from times when nature and its laws were considered a primary teacher. The distortion of this symbol via man-made religion has become half-man, half-beast (demon).

This sign reflects the dynamic of truth. In a natural expression, this will manifest as personal honesty and truthfulness. In a distorted expression, this will manifest as embellishments, exaggerations, and outright lies. The reason for this dynamic is a compensation for a sense of lack and inferiority. This is reflected in the natural square from the sign of Virgo to Sagittarius. The need to become personally honest and purge all forms of dishonesty is emphasized.

The polarity sign of Sagittarius is Gemini. The sign of Gemini corresponds with the need to collect a diversity of facts, information and data from the external environment. This sign reflects the intellect and mental expansion. It symbolizes the left brain which is logical, rational, and attempts to build the whole out of all the individual parts (deductive logic). Communication is indicated by this sign. Communication serves to process information that is collected from the external environment.

Typically, we will only take in information that supports a pre-existing view point or opinion. In other words, information that does not support the existing intellectual structure and resulting viewpoints will be considered invalid. This sign highlights the need to learn the difference between fact and opinion. In a natural expression, communication will be based upon objective facts rather than subjective viewpoints, opinions, and biases. Conversely, duplicity can take place.

The sign of Gemini symbolizes the awareness of the relativity of truth, or of the many paths that lead to the same goal. In essence, it symbolizes the natural principle of unity in diversity. The key within this is that the individual must realize that whatever they have come to identify as their own personal truth is not the truth for all. This is reflected in Gemini's polarity to Sagittarius.

In its highest form, this manifests as the capacity to communicate the diversity of expression of natural laws. For example, this can be expressed as the ability to illustrate how the same natural principles are seen within various tribes, cultures and nations; the underlying message of unity in diversity. In so doing, the intellect can be used to communicate intuitive knowledge, and a balance of the right and left brain can occur.

Now that we have reviewed the signs of Sagittarius and Gemini, we can discuss the evolutionary intentions of the South Node in Sagittarius/9th house, and the North Node in Gemini/3rd house. What is the prior life self-image of the Soul? What are the specific dynamics that represent the conscious emotional security of the past?

The South Node in Sagittarius/9th house

The South Node in Sagittarius/9th house symbolizes that the prior life self-image is based upon the need to emotionally connect with one's personal truth and intuitive development, to purge delusive beliefs, and to become personally honest. There is a sense of special destiny that is linked with the discovery of personal truth. Most often, the need to convince and convert others, and offer generalizations of personal truth, are patterns of behavior that have become outdated and are inhibiting further growth. These dynamics reflect the conscious emotional security of the past.

Coming into the life, the Soul will desire freedom and independence in order to discover its personal truth and, typically, the individual will not tolerate any restriction of the freedom to do so. Life is seen as an ongoing adventure. The self-image is buoyant, light, and the famous "silver lining" is visible within the gray clouds. The ability to laugh at oneself and the absurdity of life in general creates a psychological levity.

Commonly, honesty is highly valued. The elimination of all exaggerations, lies, and dishonesty is symbolized. Intuitive development and alignment with natural laws as reflected in the manifested Creation are central dynamics as well. These individuals will typically have a highly developed intuition that is carried over into the current life. In essence, the Soul is learning to feel the difference between that which is based in man-made belief and that which reflects natural law, or that which is inherently true. In this way, the Soul's underlying emotional structure or foundation becomes rooted in personal honesty.

The Consensus State: In the Consensus State, the South Node in Sagittarius/9th house will manifest as a prior life self-image or emotional structure that is based upon alignment with personal truth as defined by the beliefs within the mainstream society or culture of birth. Intuitive knowledge of cultural truth coming into the life is symbolized by this South Node.

The Soul will desire to advance within society through learning the underlying beliefs within the mainstream culture. For example, higher education could become a vehicle through which the Soul actualizes its personal truth and gets ahead within the system. Interpretation of others and life in general is based upon this belief system.

The individual will feel a sense of special destiny that is linked with the discovery of personal truth within a mainstream context. In a natural expression, the Soul will encourage others to discover their own personal truth within the mainstream. Conversely, some individuals will attempt to convince and convert others due to the emotional security that is derived from delusive beliefs.

The Individuated State: In the Individuated State, the South Node in Sagittarius/9th house will manifest as a prior life self-image and emotional foundation that is based upon an alignment with personal truth that is independent from the mainstream society.

The Soul will desire to liberate from the beliefs within the mainstream, and to define its personal truth from within. As such, the individual needs emotional freedom and space to explore and discover this truth without interference. Cultural alienation may be experienced in the sense of not feeling at home, and a resulting emotional restlessness. Most often, there is need to bond with like-minded others who also seek to individuate from mainstream beliefs and connect with their emotional truth from within.

The individual will feel a sense of special destiny that is linked with the discovery of personal truth that reflects their individuality. The individual will have an intuitive knowledge of metaphysical and/or philosophical principles coming into the life. In the best expression, this can manifest as an inherent ability to teach these principles to others. These Souls will then motivate others to do what they must to individuate from the beliefs and truth within the mainstream society, and discover their unique personal truth from within themselves.

The Spiritual State: In the Spiritual State, the South Node in Sagittarius/9th house will manifest as a prior life self-image and emotional structure that is based upon alignment with natural, timeless, principles as reflected in the manifested Creation. Intuitive knowledge of natural laws coming into the life is symbolized.

The individual will need emotional freedom and space to discover their personal truth through union with the Source. For example, the individual could desire to spiritually develop through being alone in nature because it provides the freedom to discover and connect with the natural laws directly. In some cases, this can be expressed as "Nature is my church."

The Soul's personal emotional truth is rooted in universal, timeless laws. These Souls will commonly be perceived as a teacher by others because of this knowledge. The Soul will then motivate others to discover their personal truth through direct experience of natural, universal principles as reflected in the totality of Creation. In other words, it inspires others to become their own "inner teacher" through developing this emotional connection with God/dess.

North Node in Gemini/3rd house

What is the evolving or forming self-image and emotional structure of the Soul? What dynamics symbolize the pull towards future? The North Node in Gemini/3rd house signifies that the forming self-image within the Soul is based upon the collection of facts, information, and data from the external environment, and communication of this information. It reflects intellectual expansion, and the resulting emotional need for diversity.

The intention is to embrace viewpoints, ideas, and information that reflect the natural principle of unity in diversity, that many paths lead to the same goal. In other words, it is to evolve out of the emotional security linked with the prism of one's subjective beliefs via the intake of new knowledge, information, and data.

To trigger this lesson, the individual will commonly experience intellectual/philosophical confrontations with those who hold beliefs that are just as powerful as their own. In essence, the need is to learn that the Soul's personal truth, whatever that truth may be, is relative.

In so doing, there will no longer be the need to convince others. Communication will become Socratic instead of indulging in the need to be right due to the emotional security that it brings. The key within this is that the Soul becomes emotionally secure enough to take in the beliefs and viewpoints that differ from its own personal truth without feeling threatened (South Node in Sagittarius/9th house, North Node in Gemini in the 3rd house).

The need to develop a language system that most people understand is symbolized by this North Node. The inherent intuitive knowledge symbolized by the South Node in Sagittarius/9th house must be communicated in a cohesive, coherent way. One potential vehicle for this emotional shift to take hold is through the use of a diversity of examples within nature to illustrate a central principle, or concept.

For instance, JWG uses the analogy of a mountain eroding over time to express the natural principle of uniform change or growth, and a volcano suddenly erupting to express the natural principle of cataclysmic growth. This evolving emotional foundation allows the intellect to be used to communicate intuitive knowledge, and a balance of the right and left brain occurs (South Node in Sagittarius/9th house, North Node in Gemini/3rd house).

Consensus State: In the Consensus State, the North Node in Gemini/3rd house will manifest as an evolving self-image and emotional structure that is based upon the collection of facts, information, and view points within the mainstream environment, and communication of this information to others. For example, the individual could absorb information from a diversity of voices of authority within a given mainstream field in order to advance within the field.

In so doing, the Soul will expand beyond the limits of its personal truth as defined by the beliefs within the mainstream culture and evolve out of a sectarian view (South Node in Sagittarius/9th, North Node in Gemini/3rd house). The pull towards the future will be felt in these ways. Conversely, the individual will not take in any information that contradicts their own beliefs or viewpoints, and will defend these views as valid. This dynamic occurs because of the emotional security linked with subjective beliefs and viewpoints.

Individuated State: In the Individuated State, the North Node in Gemini/3rd house will manifest as an evolving self-image that is based upon the collection of facts, information and viewpoints within the alternative of society, and communication of this information to others. For example, the individual may absorb information from a variety of alternative fields in order to emotionally grow past the limitations of its subjective beliefs and truth.

This will most often be felt as a growing need for diversity; to expand through the mental mind in the way already described. The individual then gains the ability to communicate intuitive knowledge that is independent from the mainstream society, and to express their personal truth. This reflects the pull towards the future. The key within this is that in whatever way it happens, the Soul will promote the view of unity in diversity rather than unity in the sameness.

Spiritual State: In the Spiritual State, the North Node in Gemini/3rd house will manifest as an evolving emotional structure that is based upon the need to collect information, view points, and data that are centered upon timeless, universal principles.

The Soul will desire to continue to spiritually develop through the intake of information from a diversity of sources within a spiritual community and/or accepted spiritual authorities. In so doing, the individual will expand upon their existing knowledge base. This facilitates the emotional shift from the subjective personal truth to timeless, or universal truth.

For example, the Soul could demonstrate that are a diversity of ways to express natural laws as reflected in a variety of spiritual teachings, writing, and practices which advocate unity in diversity. In other words, in the best expression these Souls can become powerful communicators of the intrinsic truth that there is no "one way" for all; and encourage others to embrace whatever path is most aligned with their personal truth. The pull towards the future is felt by these areas.

**Famous people with
South Node in Sagittarius/9th
house,
North Node in Gemini/3rd house:**

Jeffrey Wolf Green
David Bowie
Bjork
Eddie Vedder

South Node in Capricorn/10th house,
North Node in Cancer/4th house

Before we discuss the core evolutionary intentions of the South Node in Capricorn/10th house, and the North Node in Cancer/4th house we must review the signs of Capricorn and Cancer.

The sign of Capricorn correlates with the need to learn how society is structured and operates: the rules, norms, laws within any given culture or nation, and to establish a personal voice of authority within society. The career, or social role, can be a vehicle with which to develop a personal voice of authority within society. It symbolizes the mainstream of society, and the need to conform to its accepted social norms.

The sign of Capricorn reflects man-made laws and the resulting morals, ethics, and socially prescribed rights and wrongs. There is vast difference between man-made law and what is intrinsically right and wrong (Natural Law). The example given to us by JWG to illustrate this point is leaving a baby on the freeway. We know this is intrinsically wrong independent from any socially constructed laws or rules.

There are two different types of guilt reflected by this sign. There is acquired, or learned, guilt. This is guilt based on man-made laws, and must be jettisoned from the Soul as it inhibits evolution. There is natural guilt which is based upon our own actions. Natural guilt occurs whenever we transgress natural law. Natural guilt serves to teach us never to repeat the same mistake again.

Judgment is signified by this sign. All too often, we internalize the socially accepted standard of behavior, the rights and wrongs, in such a way that any deviation from it creates inner judgment and guilt. This is an example of learned guilt. Emotional suppression or repression then results. We then judge others based upon these same standards. However, if we internalize natural law, what is intrinsically right and wrong, then we use these principles as the basis of both internal and external judgments. In this way we can use judgment to purge acquired guilt. Judgment is intrinsic to consciousness; it is the standard that is used to form judgments - that is the critical point.

Emotional maturation and self-determination are signified here. We mature via accepting the responsibility for our own actions and in so doing can become motivated to accomplish whatever goals we set. The psychology of reflection is indicated. Reflection leads to the awareness of the dynamics that have become crystallized, outdated, and are blocking further growth. Conversely, we can blame society or others in general, and adopt the attitude that the end justifies the means. Authenticity is symbolized. In essence, we must become authentic by defining from within what is right and wrong, what constitutes reality and what does not, and our natural role in the world.

The polarity sign of Capricorn is Cancer. The sign of Cancer corresponds to the self-image of the Soul, and the inner world. This sign symbolizes conscious, or subjective, emotional security. It reflects the early childhood environment, and the mother or key female figure. As children we do not have any filter or defense against our environment; we take it in wholesale. Our ability or inability to nurture is symbolized as well. A key evolutionary intention is to learn the difference between external, and thus dependent security, and internal security. Typically, external emotional security factors are removed to trigger the lessons of self-security. For instance, one or both parents may have been unable to meet the individual's emotional needs in childhood.

As children we all expect to be nurtured and given to in the ways that we need. Children naturally cry if does not happen. When these needs are not met in early childhood displaced emotions are carried over into adult life. The underlying need is to foster emotional security through learning to meet our own emotional needs from within instead of externally. In so doing, we can then access vulnerability in a safe and healthy way. In a positive expression, the individual will promote self-nurturing and energizing self-security rather than a dependency upon external sources.

The anima/animus, or inner male/female corresponds to this sign. The Soul is both male and female, and simultaneously beyond gender. However, the Soul incarnates preponderantly in one gender. Over a great deal of evolutionary time we must integrate both the masculine and feminine. The key within this is that we must cultivate a space of inner security to express the masculine and feminine principles independent from socially prescribed gender roles.

The example that JWG uses to illustrate this point is the woman with the Moon in Aries. She will not relate to the image of the stay-at-home housewife just as a man with the Moon in Pisces will not relate to the image of a macho man. It takes great strength and courage to break from the cocoon of security and embrace the insecurity of change. For example, for a woman to walk as an equal in a world where men are revered, and for a man to show vulnerability when boys are taught not to cry.

South Node in Capricorn/10th house

What is the prior emotional structure of the Soul? What specific dynamics represent the conscious emotional security of the past? The South Node in Capricorn in the 10th house reflects a prior life personal lens that is based upon the need to learn how society is structured and operates, develop a personal voice of authority within society, and to mature emotionally. The lesson to learn the difference between what is inherently right and wrong and that which is based upon man-made law is symbolized as well. That which is intrinsically right and wrong reflects natural laws, while man-made laws reflect social conditioning/subjective judgments. The lesson of proper and improper use of authority is indicated by this sign.

Prior to the current life, the Soul has desired to learn how society is structured to manifest a personal voice of authority within society. The career or social role is a vehicle through which this actualization can take place. Most often, coming into the life, the Soul has internalized the social norms of behavior within the mainstream society of birth, and has accepted these norms as correct. Any deviation from it creates an inner sense of judgment and guilt. Emotional repression/suppression and learned guilt are patterns of the past that are inhibiting further evolution.

Commonly, the individual is given many responsibilities at an early age, and thus has had to mature quickly. In other situations, the Soul may have become a *de facto* adult in early childhood. In essence, the parent(s) projected an intense and rigid code of conduct to which the Soul was expected to conform. Within this is the fact that both situations reflect the dynamic of emotional repression/suppression. Positively responded to, reflection upon these dynamics can effect the necessary changes, and cause the elimination of learned guilt. Natural guilt that is based upon past actions will serve as a vehicle through which the individual accepts responsibility for their actions and emotionally matures. It serves to trigger the awareness of what is inherently right and wrong and so not repeat the mistakes of the past. Responsibility and determination are natural expressions of this natal South Node.

Consensus State: In the Consensus State, the South Node in Capricorn/10th house will manifest as a prior emotional structure that is based upon the need to develop a personal voice of authority within the mainstream society, and learn how society is structured. In this evolutionary state, the Soul will desire to get ahead, or on top of, the system through a socially accepted career or social role.

This requires that the individual learn and conform to the socially accepted norms and standards of behavior within the mainstream society. The Soul will expect that others also conform to the same standard of behavior, and negatively judge those who do not. The proper use of authority relative to social position is a key dynamic carried over from the past. In a natural expression, the individual will use their social role to help others learn how the system works and progress within society. In a distorted expression, the individual will use the knowledge of how the system works for manipulative purposes. This reflects the misuse of authority.

Individuated State: In the Individuated State, the South Node in Capricorn/10th house will manifest as a prior emotional structure that is based upon the need to establish a personal voice of authority within an alternative field. The Soul will desire to liberate from the socially accepted standards of behavior within the mainstream. The individual will individuate through defining what is right and wrong, and what reality is and is not, from within themselves. This is independent from culturally prescribed rights and wrongs.

The Soul will desire to actualize a career or social role that reflects the unique individuality. These individuals may have internalized guilt for not conforming to the mainstream. Such guilt must be released in order for growth to continue. The individual will bond with others of like mind who also seek to individuate, and establish themselves outside the mainstream of society. For example, this could take hold as others being perceived as voices of authority within an alternative field. In a positive expression, the individual will then encourage others to establish their own voice of authority independent from the mainstream society, and stand as a group of one if necessary.

Spiritual State: In the Spiritual State, the South Node in Capricorn/10th house is expressed as a prior life emotional structure that is based on the need to develop a personal voice of authority through merging with the Universal Source. Timeless, natural laws are the foundation upon which the Soul will actualize a voice of authority, and spiritually develop. The individual will purge learned, or conditioned guilt through alignment with such principles. In addition, the formation of judgments are based upon what is intrinsically right and wrong, independent from man-made law.

In this evolutionary state, others may perceive the individual has a spiritual voice of authority due to his or her knowledge of universal, natural laws. The Soul will desire to establish a career or social role that is centered upon service to others as a reflection of service to the Source. In a positive expression, the Soul will then use the voice of authority to help others align with a paradigm that reflects Timeless, Universal laws.

North Node in Cancer/4th house

What is the evolving emotional structure of the Soul? What are the specific dynamics that represent the shift towards to the future? The North Node in Cancer/4th house reflects a forming self lens that is based upon the need to internalize emotional security, access the emotional body, and vulnerability. In essence, it is the evolution from the external world (South Node in Capricorn/10th house) to the internal world (North Node in Cancer/4th house). Many with this nodal axis can feel as though the inner child is recovered in adult life, to grow younger as one grows older so to speak.

As the life progresses, external sources of dependencies will be released to trigger the lessons of self-security. The Soul is thrown back on itself in some way which serves to internalize emotional security. In this way, the individual will learn the difference between external and internal security.

The need to balance the responsibilities of a career, and the existing family obligations and downtime is symbolized. Additionally, reflection upon the internal structure leads to the awareness of the emotional dynamics that are in operation within the Soul, and of the self-image. Vulnerability can then be accessed in a safe way. In my view, one of the greatest lessons of the 10th house/4th house axis is that the ultimate strength lies in the vulnerability. JWG teaches that there is a healthy "adult child" in all of us no matter what our chronological age.

We can nurture ourselves and others in the ways that are needed if we energize an inner space of self-security. The integration of the anima/animus is symbolized as well. As the individual becomes self-secure, the capacity to express both the masculine and feminine principles develops. We then embrace the inner male and inner female. In so doing, we can break free from socially prescribed gender roles.

Consensus State: In the Consensus State, the North Node in Cancer/4th house will manifest as an evolving emotional structure that is based upon the need to internalize emotional security within the mainstream, and access the emotional body. The Soul will become secure and independent from the social position or career, or voices of authority within the mainstream.

For example, the individual could adhere to the social rules and regulations of a current position despite the influence of others in positions of authority who advocate manipulation of position for self-benefit. In so doing, an internalization of personal authority that comes through the social position takes hold. In so doing, an inner space of security with personal authority is energized. Conversely, some will attempt to effect emotional security through the authority and status of a social position.

Individuated State: In the Individuated State, the North Node in Cancer/4th house is expressed as an evolving self-image that is based upon the need to internalize emotional security in the context of individuation from the mainstream, and liberate the emotional body from the mainstream conditioning pattern (South Node in Capricorn, North Node in Cancer).

The Soul will desire to internalize the need for liberation independent from an external social role or voices of authority within society (South Node in Capricorn/10th house, North Node in Cancer/4th house). For example, the Soul will liberate from both internal or external sources of judgement; in this way, the individual combines the cultivation of internal security with the need to individuate. In essence, liberation occurs through the emotional body and not an external role or career. In so doing, learned guilt will be released from the Soul.

Spiritual State: In the Spiritual State, the North Node in Cancer/4th house will manifest as an evolving self-image and personal lens that is based upon the need to internalize emotional security through union with the Source. The self-image will be founded upon timeless, natural principles as reflected within the manifested Creation.

The individual will foster an emotional space of inner security independent of any specific role, or voices of authority within the spiritual community. For example, the individual cultivates inner security through internalization of the knowledge of universal, timeless principles taught within an existing spiritual organization or group. In so doing, personal authority and emotional security will not be dependent upon a specific role within a spiritual community. In a positive expression, the individual will then encourage others to internalize emotional security through union with the Source.

**Famous people with
South Node in Capricorn/10th
house,
North Node in Cancer/4th house:**

Michelle Obama

Brad Pitt

Johnny Depp

Sandra Bullock

South Node in Aquarius/11th house,
North Node Leo/5th house

In order to discuss the core evolutionary intentions of the South Node in Aquarius/11th house, and the North Node in Leo/5th house we must first review the signs of Aquarius and Leo. The sign of Aquarius corresponds with the need to individuate, and to the principle of like-mindedness.

This sign signifies the individuated unconscious which stores long term memory. This includes past life memory. The psychology of detachment and disengagement leads to a necessary objectivity. In so doing, liberation from past conditioning patterns and emotional attachments then follows. The key within this is to stand as a group of one if necessary.

There are three distinct social groups. One social group is the mainstream within society. Another social group is the alternative movement within society. There is also a social group that advocates applying a social vision of the past in modern times. This group has been termed the "social dinosaurs" within society. The Evolutionary State of the Soul will determine the social group of like-mindedness.

The sign of Aquarius symbolizes the dynamic of trauma, and the potential for post traumatic stress disorder (PTSD) as well. Trauma serves to trigger the necessary liberation from past patterns of behavior that have become crystallized and outdated. Trauma can be used positively to foster personal transformation, and to decondition from societal conditioning patterns that are inhibiting further growth. Emotional detachment allows trauma to be processed. As such, there is a cyclic need to disengage from the emotional body to facilitate the necessary liberation and objectivity.

Projections correspond to this sign. Projections manifest from the unconscious, and may be linked to unresolved trauma. In other words, the trauma of the past may be unconsciously projected into the current moment in time, which results in recreation of the trauma via the projection. The need to decondition, or deprogram, the unconscious from the impact of traumatic memories then follows.

The polarity sign of Aquarius is Leo. The sign of Leo symbolizes the need to creatively take control of the special destiny through the strength of will. It is through this sign that we become aware that we have something special to offer the world, such as a creative capacity or talent, and the desire to manifest these capacities. Most often, a pyramid reality structure is created in which our needs are at the very top, and every other contributing life factor is expected to revolve around and serve these needs. This sign also reflects a high degree of self-focus upon the creative purpose. Essentially, we can become "full" of ourselves.

The need for external validation and feedback from the environment can become constant. This dynamic manifests because Leo naturally follows the sign Cancer: egocentric insecurity. In this situation, no matter how much is given it is never really enough. Positively expressed, self-empowerment can occur as the Soul learns to validate itself from within, and is no longer dependent upon the external environment to provide this feedback.

Most commonly, the individual validates and gives to others based upon his or her subjective, or self-centered, reality. In other words, the Soul may attempt to guide the creative actualization of others based upon their own self-centered creation, or projection of the other, and give to others according to what it thinks is needed from their own subjective reality. All too often, giving only occurs relative to fulfillment of a personal need or agenda.

As the individual learns to inwardly validate him or herself from within, the need for external recognition and feedback will be purged. In so doing, the capacity to acknowledge the creative gifts of others without feeling threatened by them will take place. The Soul will then seek to motivate others to self-actualize in a way that supports the reality of others rather than their own. The true generosity symbolized within the sign of Leo can then manifest.

Now that we have reviewed the signs of Aquarius and Leo, we can discuss the core intentions of the South Node in Aquarius/11th house, North Node in Leo/5th house. What is the emotional structure of the past? What are the specific dynamics that constitute the conscious emotional security of the past?

The South Node in Aquarius/11th house

The South Node in Aquarius/11th house symbolizes that the prior life self-image is based upon the need to liberate from outdated patterns of behavior, individuate, and bond with like-minded others. Objectivity, detachment, and emotional disengagement are patterns of the past that represent conscious emotional security, and will be carried over into the current life.

Coming into the life, the individual will have the capacity to step outside of themselves, to detach from the immediacy of the subjective reality and become an observer of themselves and life in general. This South Node placement symbolizes the potential for unresolved trauma (PTSD). As such, this requires the Soul to cyclically disengage from the emotional body as this fosters the ability to liberate and decondition from past patterns that are preventing further growth.

Most often, the individual will desire to bond with those of like mind, and may have formed strong attachments to others of like mind prior to the current life. Emotional attachment(s) are released as the Soul cultivates the ability to stand as a group when necessary. In essence, the underlying need is to sever outdated emotional attachments that are creating stagnation and non-growth.

Consensus State: In the Consensus State, the South Node in Aquarius/11th house will manifest as a prior emotional structure that is based upon the need to bond with others of like mind within the mainstream, and liberate within the social strata.

The Soul will desire to advance within society through a social group or associations with others of like mind.

For example, the individual may observe existing practices and techniques within any given field in the mainstream to progress within it. Associations can be used for this same means. Liberation via progression within the social strata then follows. The individual will project that the overall lifestyle and norms of the mainstream should be followed by all. The Soul may have experienced trauma within a mainstream group of like-minded people and need to enforce the necessary liberation from past patterns that have become outdated; to sever emotional attachments that are preventing further growth.

In a natural expression, the Soul will advocate standing or bonding together within the community to create positive social change. The capacity to stand as a group of one and resist negative peer group pressure within the mainstream is essential. Conversely, it will resist this liberation and conform with the group mentality due to the emotional security that linked these social bonds and associations. In this way, trauma of the past is recycled into the future.

Individuated State: In the Individuated State, the South Node in Aquarius/11th house will manifest as a prior life self-image and personal lens that is based upon the need to bond with others of like mind within the alternative movement of society, and individuate from the mainstream society. The Soul will foster liberation through bonds with like-minded others who also seek to individuate and feel alienated from the majority of society.

The underlying need and intention is to liberate from dependencies upon any social group in an alternative field to decondition from the mainstream. For instance, the Soul may have unique and revolutionary ideas, yet not be able to manifest them within an existing social group. In addition, the individual may have suffered trauma for being different from those in the mainstream, and formed attachments with groups of like-minded others who experienced the same dynamic. These bonds may have become outdated and are preventing further growth. In the best expression, the Soul will then encourage others through example to individuate from the mainstream, and stand as a group of one if necessary.

Spiritual State: In the Spiritual State, the South Node in Aquarius/11th house is expressed as a prior emotional structure that is based upon the need to liberate and decondition through merging with the Source, and bond with like-minded others who also seek to spiritualize. Timeless, natural principles are the foundation of the community and the determinant of like-mindedness.

The underlying need and intention is to liberate from any dependency upon a spiritual group or community to spiritually develop, and stand as a group of one if necessary. The Soul may have experienced trauma within a spiritual community to trigger the necessary liberation from past patterns that are inhibiting further growth. A severing of outdated emotional attachments then follows.

Conversely, the Soul may sustain a dependency upon a spiritual community or others of like mind. For example, ideas of how to teach natural laws and principles in a transformed or unique way would fail to materialize due to the security that is linked with conforming to the group. In this way, trauma is recycled into the future.

North Node in Leo/5th house

What is the evolving emotional structure of the Soul? What are the specific dynamics that reflect the pull towards the future? The North Node in Leo/5th house symbolizes the forming self-image that is based upon creative actualization, self-empowerment, and the underlying need to take control of the special destiny through the strength of the will. These are the dynamics that represent the shift towards the future.

In essence, the intention and need is to take charge of its special destiny and manifest the unique gifts and talents independent from the influence of any social group (South Node in Aquarius/11th house, North Node in Leo in the 5th house). Self-empowerment occurs as the individual takes control of their destiny and manifests their creative capacities.

As the life progresses, the lesson is to self-actualize in a way that reflects the Soul's own sense of special purpose outside the influence of any social group of like mind. In this way, emotional attachment(s) and dependencies are eliminated. Most often, this requires a more or less subjective focus; to become "full of what we are" so to speak. In a natural expression, the individual will materialize their unique ideas without the support of any social group.

Consensus State: In the Consensus State, this will manifest as an evolving emotional structure that is based upon the need to take control of the destiny, and self-actualize within the mainstream society. The underlying need is to materialize the creative capacities within the mainstream.

In this evolutionary state, the individual will desire to get ahead of the system. Self-actualization of a unique capacity can be used to advance within the social strata. For example, the Soul may a special capacity such as speaking or writing, and can use this talent to progress within the social strata.

This emotional shift serves to promote the necessary liberation from dependencies upon social groups within the mainstream (South Node in Aquarius/11th house, North Node in Leo/5th house). Positively, the creative abilities are linked to the need to advance within the social system. Conversely, the individual will actualize in a more or less self-centered manner that reflects delusions of personal grandeur. This dynamic occurs because of the emotional security that is derived from these delusions.

Individuated State: In the Individuated State, the North Node in Leo in the 5th house will manifest as a forming emotional structure that is based upon taking charge of the special destiny and creative actualization within an alternative field.

In this evolutionary state, the underlying need and intention is to liberate from the mainstream via materialization of special gifts or talents that reflect the unique individuality. For example, the individual could have a special talent within an alternative community, such as regression therapy, or astrology. This talent can then be used to foster self-security with the need for self-actualization within an alternative field. In so doing, self-empowerment and liberation from dependencies upon any social group and like-minded others takes hold (South Node in Aquarius/11th house, North Node in Leo/5th house). In a positive expression, the Soul encourages others through their example to take charge of their destiny through manifestation of the unique and individual capacities. This pull towards the future is felt in these areas.

Spiritual State: In the Spiritual State, the North Node in Leo in the 5th house is expressed as an evolving emotional structure that is based upon the underlying emotional need to take control of the destiny and creatively actualize through union with God/dess The sense of special destiny is linked to materialization of creative abilities that reflect timeless, universal principles.

In this evolutionary state, the intention is to self-empower through self-actualization of the knowledge of natural and universal laws. In so doing, liberation from any spiritual group or organization then follows (South Node in Aquarius/11th house, North Node in Leo/5th house). In essence, the forming emotional structure and self-lens becomes a channel for the creative principle of the universe to flow. The Soul will not be attached to his or her creative abilities from an egocentric point of view. In turn, the individual will encourage others to take control of their destiny through alignment within natural laws and co-creation with the Universal Source.

**Famous people with
South Node in Aquarius/11th
house,
North Node in Leo/5th house:**

Barack Obama

Jodie Foster

Princess Diana

Mahatma Gandhi

South Node in Pisces/12th House,
North Node in Virgo/6th house

In order to discuss the intentions of the South Node in Pisces/12th house and the North Node in Virgo/6th house we must review the signs of Pisces and Virgo. The sign of Pisces corresponds with the need for ultimate meaning, to embrace a transcendent reality, and to merge with the Source of All Things. This sign reflects the culmination, or closing, of an entire evolutionary cycle. Illusions, delusions, and fantasies are symbolized as well.

The need for ultimate meaning is commonly projected externally into the relevant area of life; relationships, career, etc, in such a way that it is given total meaning. Illusions, delusions, and fantasies are created whenever ultimate meaning is projected externally in these ways.

Disillusionment is signified. Disillusionment is one of the most painful of all emotional experiences, yet in the end is serves to align us with actual reality. As such, the sign of Pisces indicates where we can become inspired by Source or are susceptible to illusions and delusions. The key within this is that ultimate meaning can only be found from within through embracing transcendent principles and cultivating a relationship with Source. In this way, we can merge the emotional body with God/dess.

A higher cause or purpose can become a vehicle to foster ultimate meaning from within the Soul. For example, volunteer, charity, and non-profit work are possible expressions of a higher cause. In essence, right work serves to align the individual with the Universal Source and to develop ultimate meaning from within. In this way, the external role, whether large or small, will not matter. The work is performed for the inner meaning that it holds, for the sake of the work itself. This signifies the intention to embrace a transcendent reality. Conversely, some can reject this intention through the dynamic of escapism. For instance, substance abuse may occur due to the need to escape reality.

The polarity sign of Pisces is Virgo. The sign of Virgo corresponds with self-improvement, self-purification, and service to the whole. In essence, we are transitioning from subjective development (Aries-Leo) to objective development (Libra-Pisces). Any dynamic that is linked with overly subjectively focus symbolized by the signs of Aries-Leo will be considered "not right" relative to the transition into objective focus symbolized by Libra-Aries. Discernment of actual reality verses the apparent reality and illusions and delusions (Pisces polarity sign) is signified.

Service to the whole is highlighted. We become aware of all our imperfections, impurities, faults, and desire to effect self-improvement relative to the need to serve the whole. Crisis is often created in order to trigger the necessary inner adjustments. Positively responded to, crisis leads to self- knowledge. In a negative expression, excessive crisis and an overly critical focus on the self leads to a state of perpetual self-undermining behavior.

In this situation, we make what appear to be logical excuses, rationalizations, as to why we are not ready or perfect enough to do the tasks we know we are capable of performing. The reason for this dynamic is that all too often there is an inner existential void that is more than an aloneness. The individual then compensates for this void through a variety of avoidance and/or denial associated behavior. For example, the busy bee syndrome can manifest in which we are always engaged in external activities and obligations.

The psychology of sado-masochism is symbolized by the sign of Virgo. The seeds of sado-masochism are contained within the Garden of Eden myth. In this myth women are presented as the spiritual downfall, or temptation, of men. Women are made to feel guilty, inferior, and the need to atone for the guilt. This reflects the pathology of the masochism. Men are made to feel guilty, superior, with the resulting need to punish, or get back at others as a reaction to the guilt. This reflects the pathology of sadism. Typically, women embody masochism while men embody sadism, however, these two psychologies can exist simultaneously, and fluctuate, within the same person. Victimization is signified here.

Now that we have reviewed the signs of Pisces and Virgo, we can discuss the core intentions of the South Node in Pisces/12th house, and the North Node in Virgo/6th house. What is the emotional structure of the past, and the specific dynamics that represent conscious emotional security of the past?

The South Node in Pisces/12th house

The South Node in Pisces/12th house reflects that the prior life self-image is based upon the need for ultimate meaning, to embrace a transcendent reality, and to merge the emotional body with the Source. The need to release illusions and delusions from the Soul is emphasized as well. Most often, these individuals will have a hyper-sensitive emotional body. An entire evolutionary cycle is coming to a close, or culmination.

Prior to the current life, the Soul may have experienced disillusionment. This dynamic occurs whenever ultimate meaning is projected externally. For instance, if ultimate meaning was given to a relationship, or a career, the individual will then experience disillusionment within this specific area. For example, if the Soul projected ultimate meaning onto a partner, and as a result did not see the partner clearly, he or she will experience the pain of disillusionment as the partner's actual reality becomes clear. One possible expression of this is what has been termed the Florence Nightingale syndrome. This describes a situation in which the individual unconditionally gives without discernment or boundary.

Commitment to a higher cause or purpose is a vehicle through which ultimate meaning is found from within. As mentioned previously, the intention of disillusionment is to re-align us with actual reality (Virgo polarity). This experience can also occur relative to the projection of ultimate ideals, or idealized standards of conduct. The key within this is to cultivate ultimate meaning from within through embracing a transcendent reality, and merging the emotional body with the Universal Source. In so doing, an evolutionary cycle is then brought to completion.

Consensus State: In the Consensus State, the South Node in Pisces/12th house reflects a prior emotional structure that is based upon the need for ultimate meaning, and to embrace a transcendent reality within the mainstream society. In this evolutionary state, the Soul will desire to get ahead of the system through commitment to a higher cause. For example, the individual may work to promote a well-known humanitarian cause in such a way that progression within the social strata occurs.

Ultimate meaning may also be sought through mainstream religion of the society of the birth. This reflects the underlying need to unite with God/dess. Conversely, some Souls will project ultimate meaning within the mainstream lifestyle which advocates social status, wealth, and temporal values due to the emotional security that it brings. An entire evolutionary cycle is coming to completion relative to the dynamics discussed above.

Individuated State: In the Individuated State, the South Node in Pisces/12th house is expressed as a prior life emotional structure that is based upon the need for ultimate meaning and to embrace a transcendent reality within an alternative field.

In this evolutionary state, the underlying emotional need is to individuate through timeless, universal principles. Alternative healing practices such as Reiki, hypnotherapy, and yoga can become vehicles through which ultimate meaning is cultivated from within. Disillusionment may be experienced with conforming to the temporal values and the overall lifestyle within the mainstream.

This serves to trigger the necessary individuation. The Soul will bond with like-minded others who also seek to individuate through timeless, universal principles and culminate conformity to the mainstream and temporal values in general. In the best expression the individual will encourage others via their example to embrace a transcendent reality that reflects their unique individuality. In so doing, an evolutionary chapter is brought to culmination in the context of the dynamics discussed previously.

Spiritual State: In the Spiritual State, the South Node in Pisces/12th house will be expressed as a prior life emotional structure that is based upon meeting the need for ultimate meaning through merging the emotional body with the eternal, and alignment with timeless, universal principles.

In this Evolutionary State, the underlying emotional need and intention is to spiritualize through natural, timeless laws. The individual may experience disillusionment relative to false spiritual teachings and teachers. The relationship with God/dess becomes the primary source through which the Soul cultivates ultimate meaning from within. Commitment to a higher cause is expressed through "right work" as directed by the Source. In the best expression, the individual will encourage others to embrace a transcendent reality through alignment with timeless, universal laws and emotional union with God/dess. In this way, an entire evolutionary cycle is brought to closure, relative to the dynamics discussed above.

North Node in Virgo/6th house

What is the evolving emotional structure of the Soul? What are the specific dynamics that represent the pull towards the future? The North Node in Virgo/6th house symbolizes that forming self-lens and emotional structure is based upon the need to serve the whole, effect self-improvement and personal humility.

The core lesson highlighted here is to discern actual reality from illusions and delusions (South Node in Pisces/12th house, North Node in Virgo/6th house). The often diffused and unfocused healing energy contained within the Pisces/12th house must find definition through the North Node in Virgo/6th house.

167

As the life evolves, the underlying need is for self-improvement and personal humility. Typically, the inverted pyramid effect is created to trigger the necessary changes. Our needs are now at the very bottom of the pyramid. For example, service to the underdogs or under-privileged is a potential expression of this current life's intention. A service-oriented social role, or line of work, can become a vehicle through which self-purification and refinement of the nebulous healing energy reflected by the South Node in Pisces/12th house takes hold. In so doing, the ability to discern actual reality from illusion and fantasy then follows.

Consensus State: In the Consensus State, the North Node in Virgo/6th house will manifest as an evolving emotional structure that is based upon service to the whole, for self-improvement, and to learn personal humility within the mainstream society.

In this evolutionary state, the Soul will desire to advance within society. Service-oriented work within the mainstream, such as helping the unprivileged improve life conditions can be used as a means to progress within the social strata. In this way, an inner space of personal humility and self improvement is energized.

The intention is to define from within what has meaning and priority in one's life and what does not: awareness of proper priorities. The ability to discern actual reality from illusions and delusions will then follow (South Node in Pisces/12th house, North Node in Virgo/6th house).

In a natural expression, the individual will advocate helping others improve their life circumstances within the mainstream as a vehicle to get ahead of the system; manifesting one's "right work" in the consensus world. The pull towards the future is felt in these areas. However, some will undermine their intrinsic healing capacities symbolized by the South Node in Pisces/12th house and perform mundane work just to get by.

Individuated State: In the Individuated State, the North Node in Virgo/6th house is expressed as an evolving emotional structure that is based upon service to the whole within an alternative field. In this evolutionary state, the underlying emotional need and intention is to individuate through a unique form of service that reflects its individuality. For instance, service to those who have been persecuted by those in the mainstream society for being different in some way may be linked with the Soul's "right work." In this way, disillusionment of the past is healed (South Node in Pisces/12th house, North Node in Virgo/6th house).

Self-improvement takes hold through liberation from any dynamic that reflects compensation to the mainstream society. In other words, the individual may be inwardly critical of the need to individuate, and undermine their unique gifts that can be used to serve others. In a positive expression, the individual will encourage others via their own example to actualize a form of work that reflects their individuality and is founded upon service to others in some way. The pull towards the future takes hold in this way.

Spiritual State: In the Spiritual State, the North Node in Virgo in the 6th house is expressed as a forming emotional structure that is based upon service to the whole through union with Source, and alignment with timeless, natural laws.

The underlying emotional need and intention is to foster an inner space of self-improvement and personal humility through spiritual development. Commonly, the individual becomes hung up on his or her imperfections, lacks and impurities. This leads to perpetual excuse-making as to why the Soul is not ready to do the work as directed by the Source.

Service to others who also desire to manifest their right work can become an avenue to resolve and heal this dynamic. In essence, the intention is to learn that the path to perfection occurs one step at a time. In so doing, an entire evolutionary cycle is brought to culmination (South Node in Pisces/12th house, North Node in Virgo/6th house). These Souls will motivate others to align with a form of service that reflects natural, timeless laws, and advocate the natural teaching that the Source itself is not perfect, rather simultaneously perfect/imperfect; in an evolving state of perfection so to speak. The emotional shift from past to future is felt in these ways.

**Famous people with
South Node in Pisces/12th house,
North Node in Virgo/6th house:**

George Clooney

Bono (U2 lead singer)

Bob Dylan

Chapter 3

Putting it All Together –
A Client Case Study

To clarify these core points let's use a simple example. A client of mine has the South Node in Cancer in the 7th house, Aquarius Moon in the 2nd house, and the North Node in Capricorn in the 1st house. She is in the 1st stage Individuated Evolutionary state which indicates that the Soul is just beginning to break away and liberate from the consensus. At the time of the consultation, she was seeking to establish herself independent from the influence of others in personal and social relationships, and also her family. The client expressed a great deal of emotional stress acting on what she was feeling instinctually drawn towards. She was a practicing therapist and she wanted to break into a new field that went against the expectations of both personal and social relationships, including her family. How will the Soul emotionally integrate and navigate the transition from the past (South Node) to the future (North Node) relative to the current moment (natal Moon)? How will the Soul secure itself through the change, and shift emotionally security from external to internal?

In order to understand how the shift away from the past to the future will take place we must first understand the Soul's self-image of the past as reflected by the South Node. What did the Soul create to materialize the evolutionary intentions of the past (Pluto)?

The Libra, 7th house archetype symbolizes the initiation of a diversity of relationships with others through which we learn by comparison and contrast with others who we are and we are not, and which realities reflect our own and which do not. This archetype signifies that a state of extremity has been reached, and that there is a need to create balance relative to it. The dynamic of equality, justice, and fair play are highlighted here. The idiom "treat others as you would like to be treated" is a guiding principle in life in general. The natural law of giving, sharing and inclusion is the highest expression of the sign of Libra.

From a prior life point of view, the South Node in the 7th house symbolizes that the Soul has created a self-lens and emotional structure that is based upon the initiation of relationships with others. The Soul evaluates its own identity through comparison and contrast with others. Most commonly, the individual has become dependent upon others within relationships in the past, and vice versa. This will be natural point of gravitation and it also indicates areas of emotional dependency that are causing further growth to be blocked.

Imbalances and inequalities are created as soon as the Soul loses touch with its identity and needs, and continually attempts to accommodate the needs and realities of others. The underlying dynamic that creates co-dependencies and extremes within relationships is the need to be needed. The principles of equality, fair play, and giving, sharing, and inclusion are emphasized within the prior life emotional structure and self-image. As such, these principles and dynamics will be strongly felt coming into the life.

Consensus State: In the Consensus State, this will manifest as a prior life self-lens and emotional structure that is based upon the initiation of relationships with others within the mainstream society. The Soul will desire to initiate relationships with others in order to gain the necessary knowledge of how society is structured and operates, and how to progress through the social strata. As the Soul progresses within this evolutionary condition it gains the capacity to guide/mentor others to learn this same knowledge. These areas reflect conscious patterns to which the individual will feel most drawn in order to feel emotionally secure.

The Soul will conform to the prevailing societal norms and expectations within relationships on both a personal and social level and will expect that others also conform to the same socially accepted standards of behavior. The Soul will only form relationships with others within the mainstream society, and will reinforce these expectations to others who do not to feel secure. In a natural expression, this will manifest as integration into the mainstream society as an equal, and the individual will advocate equal opportunity for advancement for all. In a negative expression, the Soul will attempt to secure itself through sustaining imbalances and extremities within personal and social relationships of the past.

Individuated State: In the Individuated State, this will manifest as a prior life emotional structure that is based upon the initiation of relationships with like-minded others who also desire to individuate from the mainstream society. Relationships with those who are of like mind become a vehicle through which the Soul liberates from the mainstream, and can serve as means to learn about its own identity through comparison and contrast; who shares this same inner orientation and need and who does not.

The Soul will most often highly value the principle of relativity in the context of individual needs and realities on both a personal and social level. In other words, in a natural expression, the individual will advocate that all "realities" are equal to its own even though those "realities" may be different. In a positive expression, the Soul will be highly supportive of those who are also individuating from the mainstream society as well, and emotionally relate through the dynamic of giving in these ways.

The evolutionary need is to balance the dynamic of giving and receiving within relationships in which both partners support the individuation of each other. In this way, extremes of the past can be purged.

In a negative expression, the individual will maintain the emotional imbalances and extremes linked with dependencies upon others. In this situation, the Soul may project the need for individuation within relationships in such a way that they expect to be supported by a partner who does not have the capacity to understand or meet this need.

Spiritual State: In the Spiritual State, this will manifest as a prior life self-image and emotional structure that is based upon the initiation of relationships with others who also desire to merge with the Universal Source, and to spiritualize.

In a positive expression, the Soul will achieve emotional equilibrium through union with the Source. This has the effect of counteracting past emotional security patterns linked with dependencies and extremes linked with becoming dependent upon others within relationships, or vice versa, in the context of the need to merge with the Eternal. The evolutionary need is to initiate relationships in which both partners support the spiritual development of one another instead of creating extremes and/or mutual dependencies.

These individuals will most often emotionally relate through principles of the equality of all beings within the manifested Creation, and impart the message that Creation is inherently interrelated and interdependent. In other words, we must strive to be in harmony and balance with nature, and the whole of the manifested Creation.

Moon: What current emotional structure and self-image has the Soul created? How will the Moon act as bridge between the past and the future, and become a means to achieve self-security?

The Moon in the 2nd house symbolizes that the Soul's self-image is centered within the emotional need for self-sufficiency, self-reliance, and to support oneself without the assistance of anybody else. In the best expression, emotional security is with linked with independence and the belief that "I can do it for myself."

The Soul will most often feel a cyclic need to withdraw into itself and isolate from the impact of the external environment. This is because such isolation provides emotional stability, and a means to nurture and replenish oneself and identify inner resources that can be used to effect self- sufficiency and survival.

The sign of Taurus/2nd house corresponds to the survival instinct. Within that is the procreational instinct relative to the need for survival of the species. Thus, the Soul's sexual values, needs, and its inner relationship to sexuality is reflected. As such, a natural emotional need signified by Moon in Taurus/2nd house is sexual self-reliance; to feel that one's sexual needs are not dependent upon a partner. In my view, this fosters self-worth, and an overall positive inner space in the context of how the Soul relates to its sexuality.

With Moon in Taurus/ 2nd house, the Soul will energize the shift from past to future through creating an inner space of independence, self-consolidation, and materializing one's internal resources via self-effort. In so doing, the individual will foster self-worth and a sense of being grounded.

In the context of the South Node in the 7th house, the Moon in the 2nd reflects the need to apply, via self-effort, the knowledge that is gained from the initiation of relationships, and vice versa. In this way, the Soul will internalize emotional security instead of relying on others.

The key within this is to only initiate relationships with others who share the same values as the Soul, and have the capacity to be self-sufficient within relationships (Moon in the 2nd house). The individual will evaluate through comparison and contrast (South Node in the 7th), which others can be related to, and which not. In essence, it is to learn that the Soul must only be in relationships with others where a mutually shared space of independence, equality, and nurturing positive self is at the foundation of the relationship.

Conversely, emotional security could be derived externally from sustaining co-dependent relationships with others. In this condition, the Soul will either become the vicarious extensions of the values and expectations of others, or others will live through the Soul vicariously (South Node in the 7th house, Moon in the 2nd house). The Soul will attempt to avoid its underlying insecurities and thwart further progression in the ways described.

Consensus State: In the Consensus State, this will manifest as a personal lens and self-image that are rooted in the need to identify inner resources in order to become self-sustaining within the mainstream. The individual will seek to secure themselves through manifesting resources to progress through the social strata. The key is that this is done via the Soul's own self-effort and without assistance from anybody else.

The Soul will internalize emotional security by evaluating which relationships and life work within the mainstream reflect the need for actualization of its inner resources and support non-dependence and which do not. In other words, the individual must only engage in relationships that foster the active development of self-reliance, and are in alignment with their values within the mainstream of society.

For example, relative to the South Node in the 7th house, the individual may desire to counsel others in a mainstream context, and have an innate ability to do so. With Moon in the 2nd house, the effort required to do this can becomes a means for self sustainment to occur. However, some individuals will put only the minimally required effort into maintaining work just to get by, or survive, and may live vicariously through the resources of others due to the emotional security that is linked with this dynamic.

Individuated State: In the Individuated State, this will manifest as a prior life self-image that is rooted in the need to secure oneself through manifesting inner resources that allow self-sustainment within the alternative of society. Self-security will take hold as the Soul makes the necessary effort to actualize its resources and capacities that reflect his or her individuality. This then becomes a means for liberation from the mainstream to occur. For example, the desire to counsel others may now take place within an alternative field.

The Soul must cultivate an inner space of independence from others in order to move away from the mainstream, and nurture the need for self-reliance in the ways previously described. The individual should only form relationships with others who share the same desire to liberate, and have the ability to emotionally support mutual self-sustainment and equality.

The Soul is learning to foster meaning from within itself independent from the values and overall "realities" promoted within mainstream, and self-worth in the context of its individuality. The key within this is that the individual will liberate themselves from mainstream values, and actualize inner resources that reflect their individuality (South Node in the 7th house, Moon in the 2nd house).

Spiritual State: In the Spiritual State, this will manifest as an emotional structure and self-image of the Soul that is founded on a primary inner relationship with the Source of all Things. The individual will energize an emotional space of self-reliance and independence via this primary relationship with God/dess. Self-worth is nurtured in this same way.

The Soul will cultivate self-reliance though manifesting inner resources that are in alignment with the capacity to serve God/dess, and reflect timeless, universal laws. For example, the desire to counsel would be based upon the inner knowledge of natural laws gained from spiritual development. The key point within this is that it becomes a means to internalize emotional security and secure oneself through the transition from past to future.

North Node in the 1st house: What evolving, self-lens and emotional structure will the Soul create? The North Node in the 1st house symbolizes that forming around nurturing the development of the independent voice, and fostering an emotional independence so self-discovery can occur. The need is to cultivate the capacity to ask and answer one's own questions, and strike out on one's own, independent of any relationship. The Soul will then feel secure to ask for what it needs within relationships.

Relative to the South Node in the 7th house, this will then create an inner space of emotional balance, equality and equal giving and receiving within the relationship. By nurturing mutual self-reliance within relationships (South Node in the 7th house, Moon in the 2nd house) the individual will foster the discovery of their own identity independent from any relationship. A new evolutionary cycle within relationships will then be put into motion (South Node in the 7th house, North Node in the 1st house).

The individual will learn to initiate relationships only with those who have the capacity to be mutually independent, and to actualize their own lives by their own means. Both people are able to foster emotional independence within a relationship. In this way, the need for relationships (South Node in the 7th house) and for freedom (North Node in the 1st house) are both fulfilled, and the emotional paradox linked with relationships is resolved. The underlying attitude within relationships becomes "I am here because I want to be, not because I need to be."

As this evolutionary shift occurs, the Soul attracts others who are also self-reliant (Moon in the 2nd house), and can support the emotional need for mutual independence in an equal way (South Node in the 7th house). Conversely, the individual can recreate co-dependent relationships in the future (North Node in 1st house) due to the emotional security that is linked with these relationships. Mutually co-dependent relationships then become the primary means to effect survival and emotional stability (South Node in the 7th house, Moon in the 2nd house).

Consensus State: In the Consensus State, the North Node in the 1st house will be expressed as an evolving self-lens and emotional structure rooted in the need for freedom to initiate whatever actions are deemed necessary to get ahead of the system, and develop one's independent voice within the mainstream of society. For example, the individual may feel drawn to break new ground within a given field as a reflection of the growing inward security with their own voice. This is fostered independently from any relationship and reliance upon others. (South Node in the 7th house, Moon in the 2nd house, North Node in the 1st house.)

For example, the Soul may establish a new way to counsel within the mainstream that is based upon the materialization of the inner values of self-reliance and self-worth, and encourage others to emotionally nurture themselves to manifest their own resources to advance from a societal point of view. This reflects that a new evolutionary cycle within relationships has begun.

The Soul is no longer dependent upon others within relationships to advance within the social realm. The individual is now able to identify his or her own resources (Moon in the 2nd house), and are inwardly secure with their independent voice within the mainstream (North Node in the 1st house). However, some may act to rely on the resources of others, or only make the most minimal effort necessary relative to self-sustainment. Of course, others may become dependent on the individual in the same way. The relationship dynamics of the past are then recycled into the future. This occurs because of the emotional security it provides.

Individuated State: In the Individuated State, the North Node in the 1st house will manifest as forming a self-lens and emotional structure that is rooted in the need for freedom and independence to liberate from the mainstream, and to cultivate inward security with the development of one's own unique voice within the alternative of society. For example, the individual will desire emotional freedom to generate new experiences outside the mainstream society that allow for self-discovery to occur.

In a positive expression, the Soul will nurture the need for freedom and discovery of its own voice through initiation of independent action upon the need to individuate outside of any relationship, and without waiting or asking consent from others. In so doing, the individual energies creates an inner space of freedom and independence, fosters self-security, and puts a brand new evolutionary cycle into motion.

The new cycle within relationships begins as the Soul attracts partners who share the same desire to individuate, and have the emotional courage to strike out on their own independent of any relationship. Relationships that are centered around supporting mutual self-reliance (South Node in the 7th house, Moon in the 2nd house), and the independent self-actualization of both partners (North Node in the 1st house) in the context of progressive individuation from the mainstream reflect the emotional shift from the past to the future.

Spiritual State: In the Spiritual State, the North Node in the 1st house will manifest as an evolving self-lens and emotional structure that is rooted in the need for freedom and independence to generate whatever experiences are deemed necessary to spiritually develop. For example, the Soul may desire to merge with the Source through direct experience of nature and the natural principles therein. The key within this is that spiritual development occurs through fostering inward security with the need for initiation of actions in which actual knowledge of timeless, universal laws takes hold. In essence, an emotional space of freedom and independence is created via nurturing the need to act upon whatever experiences are deemed necessary to merge with God/dess.

In a positive expression, the individual will attract partners who share the mutual desire to spiritualize, and are able to support the need to independently, spiritually develop, and cultivate a primary connection to God/dess (Moon in the 2nd house, North Node in the 1st house). In the best expression, the Soul will encourage others to do what they must in order to experience for themselves the natural, timeless laws that reflect the whole of the manifested Creation. In this way, the individual will foster the inward security and emotional courage to ask and answer their own questions independent of any relationship, spiritual group, community, or teacher. A new evolutionary cycle can begin as the Soul develops its voice through independent spiritual development (North Node in the 1st house).

To continue with our case study, let's add signs to the South Node, the Moon, and the North Node. The South Node is in Cancer in the 7th house, the Moon is in Aquarius in the 2nd house, and the North Node is in Capricorn in the 1st house. Remember that the sign "conditions" the house. How would the given signs condition the expression of this natal signature?

The South Node in Cancer in the 7th house symbolizes that the initiation of relationships occurred within the family, or others who were in the close, immediate environment. Most commonly, the individual is highly sensitive to the expectations of her or his parents, and the overall "imprint" of the early childhood environment.

Typically, the Soul became emotionally dependent upon one or both of the parents, and those within its close and personal environment. Remember that a core intention of the sign of the Cancer is to become self-secure, and in this way learn the difference between security that is external, and thus dependent, and internal security. One way that this lesson is learned is through the experience of one or both parents being emotionally unavailable, or unable to fulfill their emotional needs. As a result, displaced emotions are most often carried over into adult life.

Conversely, the Soul may create an experience of emotional suffocation in early life via the family and close, personal environment. For example, the individual may attract parents that never truly allow him or her to grow up and emotionally mature outside of their influence. Another way this can manifest is always being expected to fulfill the emotional needs of one or both parents to the exclusion of the individual's needs. In either case, it serves to support the same evolutionary lesson: to internalize emotional security and minimize expectations on others in the external environment in general.

One expression this may take is attracting others who are just as needy and insecure as the Soul itself. This is because of the emotional security that it brings. Some may attract those who desire to become emotionally dependent through creating a *defacto* counselor/counselee dynamic (South Node in the 7th house/Cancer). In essence, the Soul is compensating for its emotional vulnerability and insecurity by attracting those who are or appear to be more needy than itself. Again, the key lesson within this is to become self-secure, and to release all sources of external emotional security that are preventing further growth.

Consensus State: In the Consensus State, this will manifest as a personal lens and self-image that is rooted in conformity to the expectations of others in the family, or close and personal environment. The imprint within the family environment is based upon mainstream values, expectations, and traditional gender roles of the society of birth. This imprint will highly impact the self-lens of the Soul coming into the life (South Node in Cancer/7th house).

In a positive expression, the individual will attract a family environment that supports the development of self-security. For example, the family may encourage the Soul to foster internal emotional security within relationships through self-nurturing and establishing their own voice independent of the family environment. This would serve to promote the ongoing lessons of emotional maturation, self-determination, and autonomy (North Node in Capricorn/1st house). In a negative expression, the individual will attempt to secure themselves through the dynamic of emotional dependency within relationships due to the emotional security that it brings.

Individuated State: In the Individuated State, the individual will initiate relationships in which close bonds with others of like mind are formed. From a prior life point of view, those in the close and personal environment will most often have become a source of external emotional security, and have highly shaped the self-lens and self-image within the Soul.

The individual will then feel that they are very different from those in the majority of society, yet may not be emotionally secure with their individuality. For example, the individual will not relate to the mainstream expectations in regards to relationships and the culturally defined gender assignments of the society of birth. This could have led to a situation in which the parents were not able to fulfill or meet the Soul's emotional needs because of an inability to understand its inherent individuality.

Mutual compensation within relationships can occur as a result of an underlying insecurity with respect to the person's individuality, and displaced emotions linked with the early childhood environment. Liberation from this dynamic can take hold as the Soul internalizes emotional security and becomes secure with the growing need to individuate. The individual will then initiate relationships with others who also desire to become secure in the same way, and can mutually nurture and support the need for individuation independently. The roles within relationships then become equal and interchangeable.

Spiritual State: In the Spiritual State, the individual will initiate close, personal relationships with others who also desire to merge and know God/dess. In a positive expression, emotional security is progressively internalized via a primary relationship with the Source of All Things. The individual will use this connection as a means to self-nurture, energize an emotional space of inner security, and by extension, nurture others.

From a prior life point of view, the Soul has become dependent upon others within relationships relative to the need to spiritualize in such a way that others may have assumed the role of teacher, and vice versa. As the individual seeks to merge and unite with God/dess, self-security is cultivated, and not sought through an external relationship. Emotional balance and stability is achieved in this way.

In this evolutionary state, the Soul will begin to integrate the anima/animus dynamic (South Node in Cancer). In other words, the individual will nurture the expression of both the masculine and feminine principles in such a way that they feel secure to manifest both sides of gender equally, despite the gender they were born into.

In so doing, a state of androgyny, or of both the masculine and the feminine expressed equally within the Soul, can take place (South Node in the 7th house). These individuals can then play the role of both mother/father simultaneously, and encourage others to nurture and secure themselves inwardly in the same way.

The Moon in Aquarius in the 2nd house symbolizes the need for emotional self-reliance and self-sufficiency that will manifest through an inward space of non-attachment, objectivity, and liberation from emotional dependencies and of the past within relationships (South Node in Cancer/7th house). Emotional detachment will create the necessary objectivity and liberation from any dependency upon social groups, associations, or friendships that do not support the ongoing need to become self-reliant within relationships.

In this case, like-mindedness is in the context of the inherent values and individuality of the Soul. Security is cultivated through nurturing the need for self-reliance, liberation, and making the necessary effort to actualize inner resources that reflect the Soul's unique essence. Inward security is fostered by standing as a group of one when necessary. Liberation from emotional attachments of the past then takes place. In so doing, the Soul secures itself through the emotional shift from past to future.

The sign of Aquarius corresponds to trauma. In the context of the Moon in Aquarius and the South Node in Cancer in the 7th house, the Soul may have experienced trauma within relationships. The Soul created this experience to trigger the necessary lessons of emotional self-reliance, independence, objectivity, and to liberate from any emotional attachment that is preventing further growth. The individual is thrown back on their own resources and must learn to support themselves through such trauma (Moon in Aquarius in the 2nd house). Positively responded to, objectivity and liberation from emotional dependencies and attachments within relationships then takes hold (South Node in Cancer/7th house, Moon in Aquarius in the 2nd house).

One possible manifestation of Moon in Aquarius in the 2nd house is breaking free from others who attempt to live vicariously through the individual, and vice versa. Another variation of this theme is detaching from social groups, friendships and associations that are not in alignment with the individual's values, sense of meaning, or overall lifestyle. In this way, the Soul learns emotional self-reliance, and to define its values and meaning from within itself instead of through others in general. This reflects the progressive shift from external to internal emotional security.

Conversely, the Soul could vicariously live through others in such a way that they become mere extensions of the others' reality, and vice versa, due to the emotional security that it provides. The key within this is to become self-secure through fostering an inner space of fundamental non-attachment to any group, friendship, or personal relationship. The ability to stand as a group of one when necessary becomes a vehicle for emotional self-sustainment and self-sufficiency to manifest. The transition from the past to the future then follows.

Consensus State: In the Consensus State, Moon in Aquarius in the 2nd house will be expressed as a self-lens and emotional structure that is founded on bonds within social groups of like-minded others within the mainstream. These social groups will hold the same values as the Soul, and will most often serve as a means through which materialization of inner resources in order for progression within the social strata can occur.

The individual must make the effort to actualize resources that align with a socially relevant need within the mainstream to progress within the social strata. Internal security will be developed through emotional liberation from any dependency upon a social group or relationship, nurturing the need for self sufficiency, and the ability to develop inner resources without the assistance of others.

For example, in a positive expression, the Soul could have a capacity to unite others who have experienced inequality and injustice, and to advocate for social change in the context of inequality. This could then become a means to create self-sustainment (South Node in Cancer/7th house, Moon in Aquarius in the 2nd house) within the mainstream. In so doing, emotional security progressively shifts from external to internal. The transition from the past to the future then follows. However, some individuals may attempt to secure themselves through social groups of like mind. In this situation, the Soul will become vicarious extensions of the peer group in regards to the group's values and overall lifestyle. This is due to the emotional security it brings.

Individuated State: In the Individuated State, Moon in Aquarius in the 2nd house will manifest as a self-image and self-lens that is rooted in bonds within social groups of like minded others within the alternative of society. Most often, these social groups will highly value the need to individuate from the mainstream. In essence, the Soul is learning to break away from emotional security patterns linked with the values and socially accepted relationship types within the mainstream (South Node in Cancer in the 7th house, Moon in Aquarius in the 2nd house).

In this evolutionary condition, the Soul must liberate from any dependency upon a social group in regards to the need to individuate, and cultivate an emotional space of security with respect to its own unique values and individuality. In so doing, self-reliance and the ability to stand as a group of one if necessary takes hold. The Soul will foster non-attachment, and release from emotional attachment (s) to any social group or relationships that are creating a block towards progressive individuation.

The individual will also encourage others to do the same. It then becomes critical that the Soul makes the effort to manifest its unique inner resources within an alternative field (South Node in Cancer in the 7th house, Moon in Aquarius in the 2nd house). This reflects the progressive shift from external to internal emotional security. In this way, transition from past to future takes hold.

Spiritual State: In the Spiritual State, the Moon in Aquarius in the 2nd house will manifest through an emotional structure and self-image that is founded upon cultivating a primary relationship with the Source of All Things as a means to nurture the need for self-reliance, and to liberate from any emotional dependency upon a spiritual group, organization or community.

The Soul must make the effort to actualize inner resource(s) that are in alignment with timeless, universal principles, and relates to a socially relevant need. For example, the individual could counsel others who have experienced traumatic events using the knowledge of natural, universal laws. The individual will then attract relationships in which there is an equal desire to spiritualize, and are founded upon a mutual support of both partners becoming self-reliant within the relationship (South Node in Cancer, Moon in Aquarius in the 2nd house).

In this evolutionary state, the Soul will commonly highly value individualized spiritual communities wherein the common bond is to merge with God/dess, service to others, and alignment with natural, timeless laws. The Soul will encourage others to materialize their own unique inner resources via developing a primary relationship to the Source. By creating an inner space of non-dependence from any spiritual group, community, or relationship the Soul gains the ability to stand as a group of one when necessary, and to emotionally and physically sustain oneself.

In essence, a primary relationship with God/dess becomes a means to foster an emotional space of self-reliance, non-attachment, and objectivity. By doing so, the Soul liberates from and releases the emotional security patterns of the past described above. Emotional transition from the evolutionary past to future will be made.

North Node in Capricorn in the 1st house: How does the sign of Capricorn condition the expression of the North Node in the 1st house? Simply stated, it corresponds with the need to learn how society is structured and operates, so the development of the independent voice, the ability to ask and answer one's own questions from within, and maintain an essential freedom and independence becomes a vehicle through which a personal voice of authority within society, emotional maturation and self responsibility takes place.

Relative to the Moon in Aquarius in the 2nd house, the drive for self-sufficiency within a group or community becomes a vehicle through which the Soul strikes out on its own, develops an independent voice outside of any relationship, and becomes mature emotionally (North Node in Capricorn in the 1st house) in the process. As the Soul becomes confident enough to initiate actions that allow autonomy and self-responsibility to take hold, relationship dynamics of the past that relate to co-dependencies, extreme and vicarious living through others will be broken (South Node in Cancer in the 7th house). The transition from the past to the future then takes place. Conversely, the Soul could attempt to secure itself through the outdated social bonds and relationships described above.

Consensus State: In the Consensus State, the North Node in Capricorn in the 1st house will manifest as a forming personal lens and self-image that is rooted in the development of the independent voice within the mainstream society, and initiation actions that allow the individual to establish his or her own personal voice of authority within the mainstream. The Soul will desire to cultivate its own voice of authority through a social position or career. In so doing, the individual will become emotionally mature and responsible.

For example, in this evolutionary state, the Soul may foster its own unique, or individualized view (Moon in Aquarius in the 2nd house), using the knowledge gained from others in the family or personal environment, in regards to how society is structured and operates (South Node in Cancer in the 7th house). This occurs in such a way that the individual becomes secure with its own voice of authority within society, and advances within the social strata. This is also in the context of finding one's own voice independent from the influence of the family environment. A new evolutionary cycle is then put into motion (North Node in Capricorn in the 1st house).

Conversely, emotional security may be derived through establishing a voice of personal authority that mirrors the family's structure, and conditioning that was modeled in early childhood. In other words, the Soul will develop of voice of authority that reflects how its identity was shaped by the imprint of the family.

Individuated State: In the Individuated State, the North Node in Capricorn in the 1st house manifests as an evolving self-image and emotional structure that is rooted in the development of the independent voice within an alternative of society. The Soul will desire to nurture the need to act independently upon the individuation impulse, and establish a social role or career that is symbolic of its individuality. The individual will foster emotional maturity in such a way as to not be defined by the prescribed roles of the culture or society of birth. This includes gender roles.

The key within this is that the Soul must become independent of any social group and family environment. This will occur through cultivating an inner space of security with unique inner resources that are in alignment with a socially relevant need within an alternative field, and reflect the Soul's individuality. For instance, in this evolutionary state, the individual can nurture the need for self-reliance through emotional disengagement and liberation (Moon in Aquarius in the 2nd house), from relationships in which conformity to the values, expectations and overall lifestyle of the mainstream society are reinforced (South Node in Cancer in the 7th house).

The individual will then feel secure in regards to his or her own independent voice within an alternative field. The Soul will initiate relationships that are based upon mutual independence in regards to the need to liberate and decondition from the mainstream. In so doing, the individual will break free from the patterns of emotional compensation and co-dependency of the past symbolized by the South Node.

A new evolutionary cycle is put into motion as the Soul fosters the development its own authentic voice within society independent from the socially accepted norms, values, and expectations of the mainstream and family environment (North Node in Capricorn in the 1st house). Conversely, the Soul may attempt to derive emotional security from outdated relationships linked with mutual compensation, and social bonds of like minded people.

Spiritual State: In the Spiritual State, the North Node in Capricorn in the 1st house will manifest as a forming self-lens and emotional structure that is founded on the need for independent action in the context of spiritualization, and merge with the Source. A personal voice of authority is created as the Soul acts to spiritualize on its own terms free from any dependency upon a spiritual group, community, teacher, etc. (South Node in Cancer in the 7th house).

In essence, by cultivating an inner space of self-reliance that is independent from any spiritual group or community, and inward security to stand as a group of one if need be, (Moon in Aquarius in the 2nd house), the individual will foster the development of his or her own personal voice of authority. As such, the Soul will need emotional freedom and independence to generate whatever experiences are deemed necessary to align with timeless, natural laws, and spiritually develop (North Node in Capricorn in the 1st house).

In this evolutionary state, the Soul will begin to integrate the anima/animus. This is reflected by the South Node in Cancer in the 7th house, and the North Node in Capricorn in the 1st house. For example, the individual may play the role of both mother and father within the family environment, or assume a role within society that reflects both qualities of the masculine and feminine. This symbolizes that the individual is becoming secure enough to manifest both the inner male/inner female, or the other side of gender, in an equal and balanced way.

A new evolutionary cycle is put into motion as the Soul emotionally integrates both genders from within itself, and becomes inwardly secure to express both the masculine and feminine principles equally in the external world (South Node in Cancer/7th house, North Node in Capricorn in the 1st house). Conversely, the Soul could attempt to secure itself through outdated relationships of the past linked with spiritual groups, teachers, and the family environment as previously mentioned.

This case study is included to illustrate how the natal Moon, by house and sign locality in the birth chart, acts as a bridge from the past (South Node) to the future (North Node). It becomes a vehicle through which the Soul returns to its original root or image as created by God/dess.

The key point within this is that the personal lens and self-image reflected by the natal Moon is structured in such a way as to facilitate the emotional integration of the gravitational shift away from the dynamics of the past (South Node) that no longer support further growth towards new patterns that represent the Soul's intended future (North Node). In this way, emotional security is progressively internalized as the Soul nurtures a relationship to the Source of all things, and returns its origins.

In the example of the client, she emotionally supported herself through the change by making the necessary effort to materialize her own inner resources without any outside support from those with whom she had been in a relationship. This then led to the ability to rely on herself instead of others in general and to create an emotional space of self-reliance. She detached from outdated relationships to facilitate this emotional shift; for example, she severed old ties with those who had been of like mind and with whom she had previously had close connections. This is reflected by the South Node in Cancer in the 7th house, and the Moon in Aquarius in the 2nd house.

She ultimately broke from her previous work as a traditional therapist and began in a new field which incorporated more non-conventional practices such as hypnotherapy and application of Jungian psychology and techniques. In the context of the 1st stage individuated state, this indicates the intention to liberate from the mainstream and individuate. She expressed that this change fostered an alignment with a role in the world that reflected her values and unique nature. It became a means to support herself through becoming established in the world in a new way, free from the influence of past personal and social relationships, and so fostered a necessary emotional maturation. This is indicated by the North Node in Capricorn in the 1st house.

Chapter 4

Case Studies of Public Figures

In this chapter we will synthesize the principles discussed so far through using indepth case studies of well-known individuals. The examples are meant to illustrate how the Moon serves as a bridge from the emotional shift from the past (South Node) to the future (North Node). The Moon signifies where we will feel the pull away from the past on a daily basis. As such, it corresponds to how we will navigate the insecurity that such changes most often trigger, and cultivate a space of internal security as we release outdated emotional security patterns of the past.

We will include the various mitigating factors such as evolutionary condition, country of birth, economic state, and cultural/religious conditioning. These factors provide the necessary context for an accurate interpretation of the natal chart from an evolutionary point of view.

The first case study is Martin Luther King Jr. He is well known for his tremendous impact and influence on establishing racial and social equality for African Americans in the USA, pioneering a civil rights movement that was inspired by the principles of non-violence taught by Mahatma Gandhi.

He organized and participated in many peaceful protests and marches against the unjust laws and unequal treatment of African Americans. The movement created long-lasting change, and ultimately led to the social inclusion and integration of both Caucasian and African Americans in the USA. King, who was in the individuated state, grew up in the low/middle

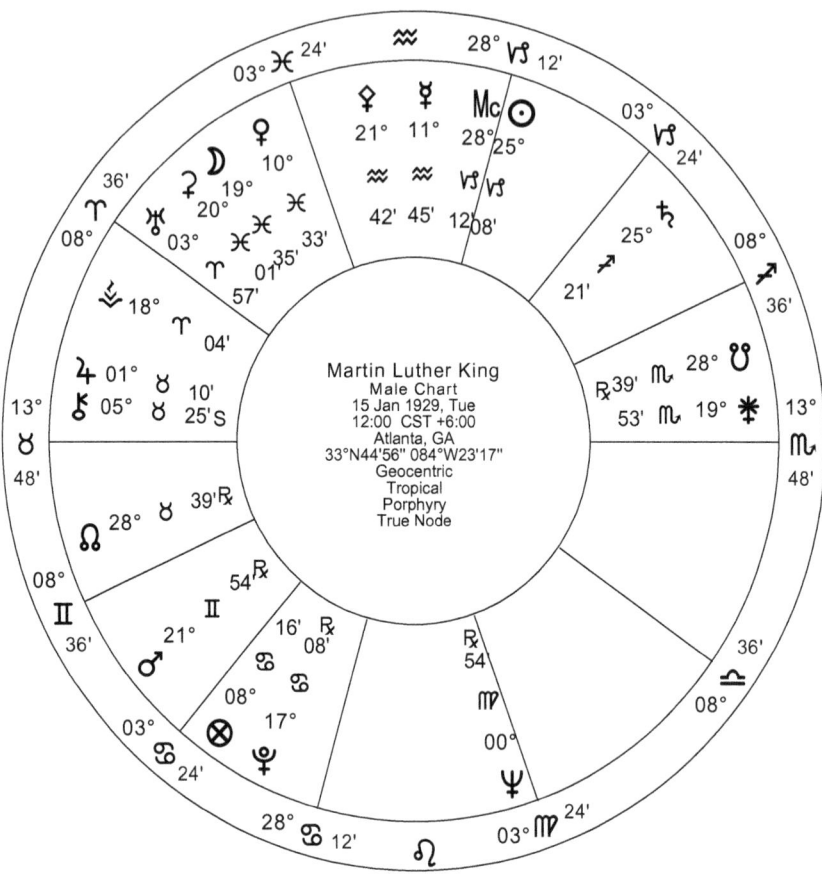

Martin Luther King
Male Chart
15 Jan 1929, Tue
12:00 CST +6:00
Atlanta, GA
33°N44'56" 084°W23'17"
Geocentric
Tropical
Porphyry
True Node

economic strata, and was raised as a southern Baptist; his father was a Baptist minister.

In his natal chart, King has Pluto retrograde in Cancer in the 3rd house, reflecting the prior life desire and orientation of the Soul to gather, collect, and communicate information from the external environment. In essence, it signifies the intention to expand through the intellect and logical mind. He is well known for his powerful and motivational speeches. In one of his most famous he passionately expressed his vision for justice, equality, and unity by embracing social integration:

"I have a dream that one day this nation will rise up and live out the true meaning of its creed: 'We hold these truths to be self-evident: that all men are created equal.' I have a dream that one day on the red hills of Georgia the sons of former slaves and the sons of former slave owners will be able to sit down together at a table of brotherhood. I have a dream that one day even the state of Mississippi, a desert state, sweltering with the heat of injustice and oppression, will be transformed into an oasis of freedom and justice. I have a dream that my four children will one day live in a nation where they will not be judged by the color of their skin but by the content of their character. I have a dream today."

Pluto in Cancer symbolizes the core intentions of the past, linked with the need to internalize emotional security, and to self-nurture. In addition, the intention is to become aware of the sources of external emotional security that are causing limitations and stagnation. In this way, the difference between security that is internal, and security that is external, thus dependent, is integrated.

As mentioned previously, King's father was a minister and deeply influential in his early life; however, during adolescence King become skeptical and rejected many of the literalist teachings of Christianity. He continued studying divinity throughout high school, going on to take systemic theology at Boston University and graduating with a PhD on June 5 1955. He worked as a Baptist minister and continued to speak out against racial segregation, advocating civil rights and social reform.

King's South Node is in Scorpio in the 7th house. The planetary ruler of the South Node is Pluto in Cancer in the 3rd house. The South Node in Scorpio re-emphasizes the power of oration and an inherent ability to communicate in a deep and transformational way. The South Node in the 7th house signifies the need for justice, equality, and fair play. He also fought for civil liberty and social justice for everyone; that all people are created equal and should be treated accordingly.

He promoted non-violent protests and peaceful civil disobedience as a means to trigger long-lasting social change, often trying to motivate others who felt disempowered by their circumstances by echoing these words of Gandhi: "do not cooperate with that which is unjust." Marching, and refusing to follow the discriminatory social policies of segregation no matter what the consequences, became a central means to protest against these policies in a nonviolent way. For example, refusing to ride in the back of a bus and give up their seat to a white passenger was one way African Americans signaled their disagreement with social inequality.

The North Node in Scorpio in the 7th house ruled by retrograde Pluto in Cancer in the 3rd reflects the questioning of information he had collected within the family environment. Specifically, questioning the literalist Christian teachings held in his father's church. In my view, this indicates an intellectual "deepening" via purging outdated mental and psychological patterns reinforced through the family and close personal environment.

In this way, an inner security developed that enabled him to sometimes disagree on a particular point where it was necessary to do so; extremes of the past indicated by the South Node in the 7th house were thus brought into balance as he confronted the limitations of his own thinking and mental patterns and spoke out against passivity. This quote illustrates this point:

"I have almost reached the regrettable conclusion that the Negro's great stumbling block in his stride toward freedom is not the White Citizen's Councilor or the Ku Klux Klanner, but the white moderate, who is more devoted to 'order' than to justice; who prefers a negative peace which is the absence of tension to a positive peace which is the presence of justice; who constantly says: "I agree with you in the goal you seek, but I cannot agree with your methods of direct action"; who paternalistically believes he can set the timetable for another man's freedom; who lives by a mythical concept of time and who constantly advises the Negro to wait for a "more convenient season."

King resisted pressure from other civil rights and African American organizations to fight back using violent methods. Rather, he encouraged others to speak out against injustice and inequality, and to demand equal rights through peaceful protests and non-cooperation with unjust laws as described previously. In my view, this is reflected in the South Node in Scorpio in the 7th house, ruled by retrograde Pluto in Cancer in the 3rd house. King stayed committed to the path of non-violent practices to effect long-lasting social change despite the insistence of some that unless more force was used no change would occur.

Pluto's polarity point is in Capricorn in the 9th house. The North Node is in Taurus in the 1st house. The planetary ruler of the North Node is Venus in Pisces in the 11th house, and the Moon is in Pisces in the 11th house, trine natal Pluto in Cancer in the 3rd house.

The 9th house polarity point reflects the current life's intentions to develop the intuitive faculty, align with one's personal truth, and focus on the deeper meaning, or "truth," of the all the collected facts. The key lesson here is that the intellect in and of itself does not know what is true and not true; this is a function of the intuition. In so doing, a holistic understanding of all the facts takes hold, and the ability to discern that which is true and that which is false is gained.

The Capricorn polarity point symbolizes the current life intentions to establish one's personal authority, accept responsibility for one's own actions, and in so doing mature emotionally. Typically, the social role or career is a vehicle through which the Soul manifests its personal voice of authority in the world. In addition, the polarity point requires the individual to develop a reflective consciousness that is centered in accepting the responsibility in one's own actions and life conditions.

In this case, King rejected the literalist Christian teachings of his father's church, and established a social role that reflected his personal truth and vision of social equality, inclusion, non-violence, and justice. In this way, he actualized a voice of personal authority in society. This social role allowed the necessary emotional maturation and development of the intuition to take hold.

His social role became a means to align with natural law, and to teach universal, natural principles to others. For example, through his role as a Baptist minister he taught the natural consequence of one extreme leading to the next extreme in the context of using violent methods to fight discrimination, and the inherent equality of all people, classes, races, etc. This is indicated in the South Node in Scorpio in the 7th house, ruled by Pluto retrograde in Cancer/3rd house. He advocated that we all have a responsibility to speak out against injustice and not cooperate with unjust laws. He is quoted as saying "Injustice anywhere is a threat to justice everywhere, and, in the end, we will remember not the words of our enemies, but the silence of our friends."

In the natal chart, the Moon in Pisces in the 11th house trines Pluto retrograde in Cancer/3rd house. In my view, this reflects the metamorphosis of the emotional structure and personal lens as he progressively identified with a higher cause or purpose. For example, as he became centered on civil rights and spear-headed the nonviolent protests and marches for civil justice he emotionally disengaged from the role of a minster, from an egocentric point of view.

King linked himself with a collective, humanitarian cause as a means to align with universal, natural law as signified by the Moon in Pisces/11th house. The trine to Pluto in Cancer in the 3rd house reflects the transformation of the self-image and emotional structure as the shift is made to embrace larger and larger frameworks; to merge with God/

dess through alignment with a universal or higher purpose. In this case, the personal identification with his role dissolved as he associated himself with a relevant social movement: civil rights and justice. The cause itself became central rather than his personal role, which triggered the necessary liberation and culmination of outdated emotional attachments.

The trine also reflects the progressive shift towards internal security to communicate his ideas and information of a universal, timeless nature. For instance, through his advocacy of equality, justice, and civil rights King vocalized the need to effect change in peaceful, nonviolent ways. He often quoted Gandhi as saying "an eye for an eye will make this world blind." In my view, this reflects the natural law that two wrongs do not make a right.

The Moon trine Pluto signifies that a traumatic event served to catalyze the necessary growth and transmutation of dynamics linked with the past that were creating limitations and blocks. In essence, it triggered the evolution from personal identification as a minster and his role within the family. For example, he spoke out against keeping silent about violence towards people of color, and promoted direct action when a bomb was set off in an African American church. The bomb killed three children, and sparked an outcry for justice within the community.

However, King didn't address the negative consequences of retaliation and violence. Instead, he began to break new ground in the fight for civil rights through initiating peaceful protests and boycotts against unjust practices. He motivated others to act in these ways via impassioned speeches about courage, justice, and freedom. For instance, he communicated that remaining silent or hidden for self-protection could no longer be justified by saying "A man has not lived until he knows what he will die for."

The Moon in the 11th house indicates liberation and deconditioning from outdated and crystallized patterns of behavior. King disassociated from other African American groups that sought to retaliate against injustices through violence. In my view, this reflects the liberation from emotional bonds and dependencies of the past.

A key lesson within this is to stand as a group of one if necessary. In the context of the Moon in the 11th house this manifests as the shift from past to the future taking place through progressive individuation, liberation from outdated emotional bonds, and cyclic emotional disengagement or detachment to gain objectivity and process traumatic experiences.

The sign of Aquarius symbolizes the need to objectify a dynamic as a means to promote liberation and deconditioning. Emotional shocks and traumas often trigger the necessary liberation and objectivity required for growth. For instance, the traumatic event of the church bombing motivated King to align with a higher cause and purpose instead of his previous personal identification as a minister. In this way, he cultivated the emotional security that enabled him to act alone.

The North Node is in Taurus in the 1st house, symbolizing that the evolving emotional structure is rooted in the need for freedom, independence, and self-discovery. The underlying intention is to ask and answer its own questions from within. The resulting emotional need is to initiate one's own life direction independent from any relationship, and to take the lead without waiting for others to act first. In this way, co-dependencies and imbalances in relationships are overcome, and overall orientation of mutual independence and co-equality is fostered.

King broke out of outdated relationships pattern by speaking his own truth when his wife asked him to step down from his role in the civil rights movement in order to ensure his own safety and survival. She emphasized that he had a responsibility to provide and care for his family first and foremost. King countered this expectation by stating that the current social conditions necessitated a new approach rather than just maintaining one's survival. He wanted to fight for a better future for his own children and African Americans by pioneering the non-violent demonstrations and boycotts. Clearly, this put King and his family in danger of being targeted by those who wanted to sustain segregation. However, he made a decision to spearhead the civil rights movement because of the long lasting impact he felt it could achieve; true change.

With respect to the North Node in the 1st house, the Soul must initiate experiences in which actualization of inherent inner resources takes hold. In so doing, consolidation and development of the independent voice is energized; King achieved this by spear-heading the civil rights movement in a way that aligned with his inner essence and values.

As mentioned previously, as he liberated from outdated emotional patterns and attachments and stood as a group of one, he progressively established connections with like-minded others within the community; this is also indicated by the Moon in Pisces/11th house.

The planetary ruler of the North Node is Venus in Pisces in the 11th house, which reiterates the themes of liberation, standing as a group of one if necessary, and aligning with timeless, natural laws. In essence, this symbolizes that as King's inner relationship became defined by his connection to the Source, or God/dess, he gained the capacity to strike out on his own and become self-reliant.

The next example is the well known primatologist Jane Goodall. She was a pioneer in the field of primatology through her work with the chimpanzees in Africa. She was born into a middle class family, had no specific religious/cultural conditioning, and was in the individuated state.

In her natal chart, she has retrograde Pluto in Cancer in the 8th house, the South Node is in Leo in the 8th house, and the planetary ruler of the South Node is the Sun in Aries in the 4th house conjunct Mars. The Moon is in Sagittarius in the 12th house. Pluto's polarity point is in Capricorn in the 2nd house, the North Node is in Aquarius in the 2nd house. The planetary ruler is Uranus in Aries in the 5th house. Uranus is square Pluto.

Natal Pluto in the 8th house symbolizes that prior to the current life the Soul has desired to transmute current limitations, gain a psychological understanding in general, i.e, the "why" of things, and to merge with a

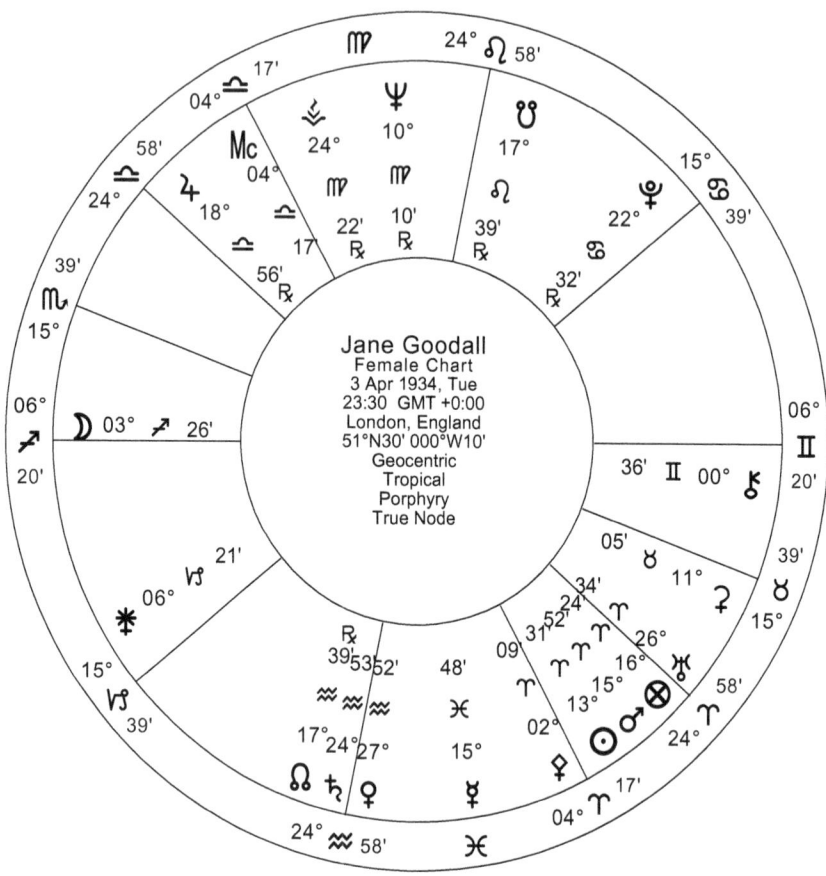

higher source of power. Within this, experiences of power and powerlessness are signified, and the natural limitations of one's own personal power.

The dynamic of abandonment, betrayal, and loss is highlighted. The underlying causes for this are based upon knowing who to trust and who not to, and there is a need to release all sources of dependency. In essence, the intention is to expose the Soul to its underlying psychology and purge all ulterior motives, agendas, and patterns of manipulation. The need is to merge with higher a source of power in such a way that personal growth and a metamorphosis of limitations then follows. This is where the Soul "left off" and will naturally "pick up" again coming into the current life.

Pluto in Cancer symbolizes that limitations of the past are linked with external emotional security factors, the need to progressively internalize emotional security, and to purge outdated emotional responses. The 8th house Pluto intensifies, or magnifies, these lessons, and re-iterates the core intention to cultivate self-security. Most commonly, the Soul "programs" situations which serve to trigger this lesson through a release of external sources. The Soul develops, then gains the capacity to self-nurture, and to transmute past patterns that are causing blocks and stagnation.

From a very young age, Goodall felt a deep connection with plants, animals and the natural world. In fact, she describes how she was most at home in the natural world, and felt alienated from the vast majority of society. She nurtured herself primarily via this connection, and in so doing transmuted the outdated emotional patterns of external emotional security. In essence, she shifted emotional security from the external to the internal as she developed her relationship with nature and the Universal Source.

This is signified by the Moon in Sagittarius in the 12th house, in the context of the South Node in Leo in the 8th house and the planetary ruler of the South Node, the Sun, in Aries in the 4th house. This reflects her connection to nature and God/dess as providing a central means to cultivate an emotional space of inner security and express her natural voice/ truth: She says, "the least I can do is speak out for those who cannot speak for themselves."

In the context of the South Node in Leo in the 8th house, the creative purpose is linked with her knowledge of psychology that transcends the current mainstream understanding of primates and wildlife in general. Specifically, she documented their capacity to invent and use tools which prior to that time had been undocumented by any existing research. This, of course, was a ground-breaking discovery that dramatically changed the prevailing views and attitudes towards primates and animals.

She cited different examples that indicate that primates have emotions, and can experience pain, joy, etc. just as humans do. For instance, she describes observing a chimpanzee which had just lost her baby; the mother carried the body of her baby for almost a week until she was finally able to separate from it. Goodall writes that the mother's emotional response seemed similar to the grief that we feel when experiencing a loss. In other words, Goodall provided examples of real life stories in which the chimpanzees expressed emotions and demonstrated that they have emotional lives. This, in turn, became a vehicle for her to open up to and access her own emotional nature. This is highlighted in her natal chart by natal retrograde Pluto in Cancer in the 8th house and the Moon in Sagittarius in the 12th house.

The dynamic for self-empowerment and self actualization is signified by the South Node in Leo in the 8th house. The intention is to take charge of the special purpose/destiny and shape it out of the strength of the will. The planetary ruler of the South Node is the Sun in Aries in the 4th house. This symbolizes that a new evolutionary cycle has just began, and the need for freedom and independence to discover what the new cycle is about. Self-discovery then follows as the Soul initiates the necessary actions to put the new cycle into motion.

Mars is in a new phase conjunction with the Sun, and in the same house and sign. This emphasizes that a new evolutionary cycle has just began. The dynamics of self-discovery and the need for freedom and independence to initiate whatever actions are necessary for the Soul to discover what the new direction/cycle is about are reiterated. In so doing, new dimensions and aspects of the individual are discovered, and Goodall moves forward from the past.

The Sun in the 4th house highlights the need to internalize emotional security, self-nurture, and to release external sources of emotional security that are preventing growth. Relative to the South Node in Leo in the 8th house, there is a need to self-validate and eliminate the outdated psychological patterns as previously described. Goodall had a deep emotional bond with her mother Val, who supported and nurtured her daughter's love of nature and wild life from early childhood. In fact, Val accompanied her to Gombe as a volunteer to assist in the research. This relationship served to facilitate the lessons of self-security and self-empowerment signified by the South Node in Leo in the 8th house and Sun in Aries in the 4th house.

Pluto's polarity point is in Capricorn in the 2nd house. The North Node is in Aquarius in the 2nd house, conjunct Saturn. The planetary ruler is Uranus in Aries in the 5th house which squares natal Pluto.

Pluto's polarity point in the 2nd house symbolizes the need to foster self-reliance, independence, and self-consolidation. The key here is to materialize the inner resources for self-sustainment and survival purposes. In so doing, an essential simplification of the overall life takes hold. Most commonly, the individual is thrown back on themselves in some way to trigger these lessons.

In this case, prior to her expedition Goodall worked as a secretary to support herself as her family had limited means and could not afford to send her to university. When she went to Gombe she described her great joy in the simplicity of the lifestyle. For example, she woke in the early morning to observe the chimpanzees and did not leave for the day until close to dusk when the sun would begin to set. This allowed Goodall to develop her research and new skills. The materialization of her inner resources became a means for self-sustainment. There were funding issues during the expedition which almost threatened to end the research altogether, however, Goodall remained steadfast in her work and documented her findings in order for the funding to continue.

Pluto's polarity point is in Capricorn. This signifies that self-reliance, actualization of inner resources, self-sustainment and consolidation are cultivated through establishing a personal voice of authority and determination. Within this, an essential maturation takes hold via accepting the responsibility for one's own actions.

As mentioned previously, Goodall stayed focused, determined and utilized all available resources to ensure that the work could continue.

In so doing, she developed a personal voice of authority and gained emotional maturity. She founded the Goodall Institute which promotes the conservation of the natural world, and fights to protect the rights of chimpanzees. Their stated mission is: "We are a global community conservation organization that advances the vision and work of Dr. Jane Goodall. By protecting chimpanzees and inspiring people to conserve the natural world we all share, we improve the lives of people, animals, and the environment."

The North Node is in Aquarius in the 2nd house conjunct Saturn, highlighting the current life lessons of self-reliance, consolidation, and materialization. Goodall's inner relationship with herself radically changed as her lifestyle became more simplified in order to complete her research.

Relative to the South Node in Aquarius, she describes liberation from outdated emotional and mental patterns resulting from the overall simplification of her lifestyle, and the experience of progressively becoming an established authority in the field of primatology. Saturn conjunct the North Node signifies the intention to become established based upon a unique and individualized body of work that is in the alternative of society. In the context of the third stage individuated state, this body of work can then serve to help the mainstream evolve over time.

For example, she documented a ground-breaking discovery that chimpanzees can invent and use tools. This discovery clearly changed the prevailing mainstream view that only humans had this capacity and intelligence. It is illustrated in the quote "I had been told from school onwards that the best definition of a human being was man the tool-maker - yet I had just watched a chimp tool-maker in action. I remember that day as vividly as if it was yesterday."

A core point within this is that the strength of her work is founded upon natural science, based upon observation and correlation rather than theory, indoctrination or belief. A central aspect of the creative actualization process is linked with teaching or imparting knowledge of universal/

natural laws in an objective way; through simply presenting her findings and documenting what she witnessed while observing the chimpanzees in an undisturbed/natural state. This is indicated by the South Node in Leo in the 8th house, the natal Moon in Sagittarius in the 12th house, and the North Node in Aquarius in the 2nd house.

Goodall had no formal university training, so did not rely on or refer to the prevailing accepted theories, but rather observed and reported her observations in an objective way. She became an established authority based upon this alternative and ground-breaking research. This is indicated by Pluto's polarity point in Capricorn in the 2nd house, and North Node in Aquarius in the 2nd house conjunct Saturn.

In the context of the natal Moon in Sagittarius in the 12th house, immersion in the natural world and her work living with the chimpanzees in Africa became a means for her to take charge of her destiny, self-empower (South Node in Leo in the 8th house) internalize emotional security and ultimately teach knowledge of natural/universal laws (Moon in Sagittarius in the 12th house) in a unique and revolutionary way (North Node in Aquarius in the 2nd house). The transition from past to future takes hold through nurturing the connection to the natural world and internalizing emotional security via cultivating a relationship with the Universal Source, or God/dess (Moon in Sagittarius in the 12th house).

An example of a well-known inspirational figure in the individuated state is Amelia Earhart, the American aviator, pioneer and author. She was the first woman to obtain an aviator's license, and fly solo across the Atlantic and across the U.S. She at first intended to become a nurse and attended Columbia pre-med school for a year. She ultimately dropped out when she made her first flight and instead decided to pursue her love of aviation. She was of low/middle economic status, and grew up with very conventional and strict grandparents, a repressed mother, and alcoholic father.

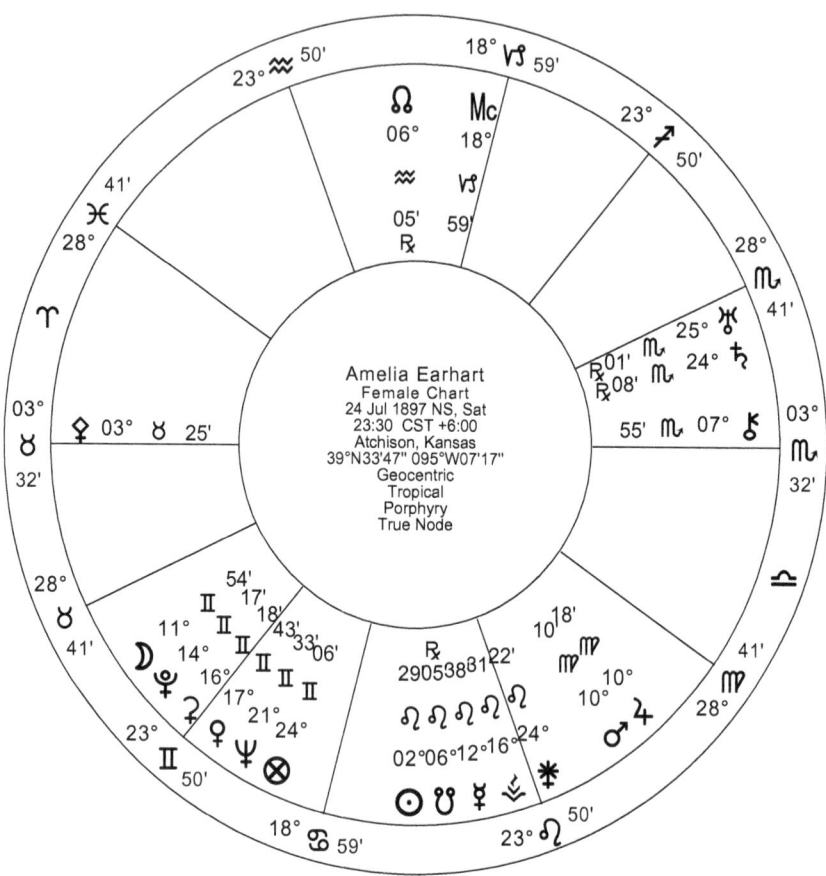

In her natal chart she has Pluto in Gemini in the 2nd house conjunct the Moon, Venus and Neptune. The Moon is in a balsamic conjunction with Pluto, and Venus and Neptune are in a new phase with Pluto. The South Node is in Leo in the 4th house conjunct the Sun which is the planetary ruler of the South Node. Pluto's polarity point is in Sagittarius in the 8th house, and the North Node is in Aquarius in the 10th house. The planetary ruler of the North Node is retrograde Uranus in Scorpio in the 7th house in a balsamic conjunction with Saturn in the same house and sign.

Pluto in the 2nd house signifies core intentions of self-sufficiency, self-sustainment, and independence. The Soul is learning to identify its own inner resources to cultivate self-reliance. Most often, the Soul creates situations in which it is thrown back upon itself in some way to trigger these core intentions.

Pluto in Gemini corresponds to the need to expand through intellectual development, and as a result collect a variety of information, data, and facts. In essence, through self-consolidation and withdrawing from the impact of the external environment Earhart can determine what information in the environment to take in and which to leave out: "what can I relate to and what can I not?" In this way, she can communicate information that is unique and reflects her root or essence.

Earhart naturally thought in new and innovative ways. This is reflected by the evolutionary state of the third individuated stage, and natal Uranus retrograde conjunct Saturn retrograde in Scorpio in the 7th house. Pluto in the 2nd house highlights the inner relationship with the self, and what we value. The intention of the 3rd stage is to integrate the Soul's genius and unique capacities in the mainstream in such a way that it helps the mainstream evolve and advance.

For example, Amelia deeply valued gender equality and became a champion for the under-privileged. This can be seen by natal Jupiter conjunct Mars in Virgo in the 5th house, and Uranus retrograde conjunct Saturn retrograde in Scorpio in the 7th house. A central message within this is to not limit one's intrinsic capacities based on conventional gender roles. In other words, both men and women are inherently equal and have equal capacities, and we should not limit ourselves based upon our gender. As such, she advocated that women be given the same opportunities to materialize their potential as men. An inspiring quote of hers that illustrates this inner orientation is: "Everyone has oceans to fly, if they have the heart to do it."

The South Node is in Leo in the 4th house conjunct the Sun, which is the planetary ruler of the South Node. This emphasizes the dynamic of self-actualization and self-empowerment. It signifies that, prior to the current life, she desired to take control of her destiny through manifestation of her special gifts and capacities. In addition, she felt a sense of special destiny linked with encouraging others to actualize themselves independently from social norms and gender assignment, to follow their passion, no matter the opinions or prevailing mainstream mentality. This was a natural point of gravitation coming into the life.

As mentioned previously, she was naturally able to help others think in new ways, to decondition from prevailing social norms, and to be free from the shackles in their own lives. This is reflected by Pluto, Venus, Neptune and the Moon in Gemini in the 2nd house, and the nodal axis in Leo (4th house) and Aquarius (10th house). She was a pioneer in fields that were traditionally considered men's, and as the first female aviator, she championed other women who wanted to do the same.

The Moon is in a balsamic conjunction with Pluto in Gemini in the 2nd house. This intensifies the core dynamics of self-reliance, self-consolidation, and materialization of inner resources to cultivate self-sustainment. The culmination of outdated mental and emotional security patterns is signified.

The transition from the past to future will take hold via cultivating an emotional space of self-reliance, self-consolidation, and inner security to communicate new ways of thinking. These new ideas promote breaking free from outdated inner relationship patterns linked with gender assignment and prevailing social norms.

For example, she said: "I believe that a girl should not do what she thinks she should do, but should find out through experience what she wants to do," and: "Women must try to do things as men have tried. When they fail, their failure must be but a challenge to others." In my view, this reflects the message of equality of gender, and that we all must have the courage to take charge of our destiny to manifest our full potential. In other words, it is not about proving to others what one can do, rather that one not be defined by cultural/social ideas and attitudes about one's abilities and appropriate social role.

The shift from external to internal security took hold as Earhart used her natural skill and capacity for aviation, and writing as a means to convey non-conventional and innovative thought patterns intended to help others liberate from unnecessary limitations in their lives. This reflects a new mind set which fostered the development of self-security and the resulting ability to pioneer and create new pathways. In these ways, she became a role model to others who also desired to liberate themselves in these same ways. In so doing, Earhart set new trends for the future. This is signified by the North Node in Aquarius in the 10th house, ruled by Uranus Rx in Scorpio conjunct Saturn Rx in the same house and sign.

One way this was expressed is in her relationship and marriage to George Putnum. Amelia communicated to him that they were equal partners within the relationship, and demonstrated this by keeping her own name when they married - which was considered radical at the time. In my view, she played a unique and transformational role which is signified by the North Node in Aquarius in the 10th house.

Pluto's polarity point in Sagittarius is in the 8th house. The North Node is in Aquarius in the 10th house, and the planetary ruler is retrograde Uranus in Scorpio in the 7th house conjunct Saturn in the same house and sign. Pluto's polarity point in the 8th house reflects the evolution from an understanding of the "how," the nuts and bolts, to the "why" of things.

It symbolizes the current life's intention to embrace deeper levels of awareness and as such, the Soul will progressively develop a psychological understanding of life in general. In so doing, a necessary metamorphosis beyond current limitations takes hold, and a "deepening" within the Soul results from this growth. In essence, the individual is exposed to his or her limitations in order to grow past them. In so doing, intuitive development and alignment with both personal truth and natural law occurs, symbolized by Pluto's polarity point in Sagittarius. In this way, a cohesive and holistic interpretation of all the facts is gained.

As Amelia purged the outdated mental and inner relationship patterns previously described, a culmination of an evolutionary cycle occurred, and emotional security progressively became internalized. Liberation and deconditioning then took hold, and the ability to manifest a unique role that reflected her individuality was gained. This is indicated by Pluto's balsamic conjunction with the Moon in Gemini in the 2nd house, in the context of the South Node in Leo (4th house) and the North Node in Aquarius (10th house).

The integration of the masculine and the feminine is signified by the South Node in the 4th house and the North Node in the 10th house. The planetary ruler of the North Node is Uranus in the 7th house which emphasizes the need to actualize both sides of gender, both the masculine and feminine, equally from within herself. In my view, this is reflected in her relationship with Putman in that she describes the marriage as a partnership in which the roles are equal and interchangeable. These became the central dynamics through which she transmuted limitations of the past, developed a psychological understanding of life in general, and aligned with her personal truth relative to Pluto's polarity point in Sagittarius in the 8th house.

Also by Deva Green

Evolutionary Astrology - Pluto and your Karmic Mission

Edited by Deva Green

(from the previously unpublished lectures of Jeffrey Wolf Green)
Essays on Evolutionary Astrology: The Evolutionary Journey of the Soul

And by Jeffrey Wolf Green

Pluto Volume I – The Evolutionary Journey of the Soul
Pluto Volume II - The Soul's Evolution Through Relationships

JEFFREY WOLF GREEN
SCHOOL OF
EVOLUTIONARY ASTROLOGY

If you are interested in learning more
about Evolutionary Astrology
please visit:

www.schoolofevolutionaryastrology.com